CORPVS MONVMENTORVM
RELIGIONIS DEI MENIS
(CMRDM)
II
THE COINS AND GEMS

ÉTUDES PRÉLIMINAIRES
AUX RELIGIONS ORIENTALES
DANS L'EMPIRE ROMAIN

PUBLIÉES PAR

M. J. VERMASEREN

TOME DIX-NEUVIÈME

EUGENE N. LANE

CORPVS MONVMENTORVM
RELIGIONIS DEI MENIS
(CMRDM)

II

THE COINS AND GEMS

LEIDEN
E. J. BRILL
1975

EUGENE N. LANE

CORPVS MONVMENTORVM RELIGIONIS DEI MENIS
(CMRDM)

II

THE COINS AND GEMS

WITH 72 PLATES AND ONE MAP

LEIDEN
E. J. BRILL
1975

ISBN 90 04 04207 5

Copyright 1975 by E. J. Brill, Leiden, Netherlands

All rights reserved. No part of this book may be reproduced or translated in any form, by print, photoprint, microfilm, microfiche or any other means without written permission from the publisher

PRINTED IN THE NETHERLANDS

Uxori patientissimae
et
amicis Atheniensibus

CONTENTS

Preface IX

Coins I

Gems 164

Addenda and Corrigenda to Volume I 170

Plates I-LXIV, plates to Addenda and folding Map at the end of the book

PREFACE

In the first volume of the *Corpus Monumentorum Religionis Dei Menis*, I endeavored to make as complete a collection as possible of the epigraphic evidence for the cult of the god Men. In this volume I will attempt to do the same for the numismatic evidence. But there are considerable differences in the nature of the evidence, and this necessarily entails considerable differences in procedure.

Coins are different from inscriptions in that they are not each one unique, but issued in quantity. Yet, right after we say that coins are not unique, we must admit that no two ancient coins are quite identical to each other. The relatively short life of dies in antiquity; the variation in weight, flan-size, and position when the coins were originally struck, together with the accidents of preservation which have befallen the coins over a period of almost two thousand years, have all resulted in individual uniqueness existing within a structure of mass-issue.

To cope with this situation in composing a corpus of the numismatic evidence for Men, remembering that our prime concern is to be historians of religion, rather than numismatists, certain arbitrary decisions are necessary. If I endeavoured to list every known specimen of every known coin, I doubt if I could ever complete the work satisfactorily. Therefore I have chosen to abide by the rather subjective concept of "issues," lumping together coins that differ only slightly in weight, size, style of representation, or inscription. This last, particularly, may be real or only apparent, as accidents of preservation easily result in the inscription appearing to be different even in two examples of a coin struck with the same die. I am not attempting a complete study of the sizes and weights of all known copies of the coins treated here. The size can be easily judged from the illustrations provided. In addition, wherever possible, I give the weight of at least one typical example of each coin. Weights of Greek imperial coins are, of course, highly variable, and the figure is merely given in order to present a rough indication of the denomination of the coin we are dealing with. In the case of a coin with an exceptional weight-range and in some other cases, I give the highest and lowest weights that I know of.

Coins, too, are an even greater bibliographical impossibility than are inscriptions. There are two particular problem areas: a) the older publications, prior to ca. 1850 (even the old standard, Mionnet, is very frustrating to use), and b) the sales-catalogues.

a) The older publications are without photographic documentation, hard to get at in libraries, and often quite inaccurate. To track down every reference to them would be immensely time-consuming, and yield relatively trivial results. Consequently I have not made any attempt to review consistently all references in Drexler's article s.v. *Men* in Roschers *Lexikon*. I include in the bibliographies only titles which I have had the opportunity to inspect for myself, and which I feel contribute valuable information to the study of the particular coin. The reader interested in the often inaccurate reporting of Men-coins in older publications is referred to Drexler's article, which, by and large, gives a reliable survey of the scholarship preceding its own time.

b) The sales-catalogues too pose a problem. Not only are they hard to get at in libraries, but they vary immensely in quality, from the productions of such firms as Münzen und Medaillen, Basel, reasonably well-researched, and excellently illustrated, to lists which give the user only the sketchiest idea of what coin exactly is for sale. Faced with this situation, I include references to sales catalogues only when they are the only or among the few references to a given coin. Even at that, I include references only to the more reliable catalogues.

It is just about impossible, even with the best intentions of completeness, to be sure that one has covered all the relevant bibliography on a given item. Therefore when I write "Bibliography: none" in the following pages, this of course means that there is no reliable bibliography of the past 100 years or so which has come to my attention. I welcome readers drawing my attention to bibliographical and other omissions.

As to the geographical order followed in this catalogue, it is according to the areas of Asia Minor into which museum catalogues are usually divided, and within each of those, alphabetically.

Specifically, the order is Pontus, Paphlagonia, Bithynia, Aeolis, Ionia, Lydia, Caria, Phrygia, Pisidia, Galatia, and Syria.

This preface would not be complete without a list of those who have helped make it possible. My thanks for their cooperation go to the National Numismatic Museum of Athens, and particularly Mrs. Oikonomidou; the Istanbul Arkeoloji Müzeleri and Nekriman Olcay; the Staatliche Münzsammlung, Munich, and Dr. Bruno Overbeck; the Kunsthistorisches Museum, Vienna, and Dr. G. Dembsky; the Bibliothèque Nationale, Paris, and Mme. Nicolet; the Staatliche Museen, East Berlin, and Herr und Frau Schultz; the British Museum, London, and Mr. Martin Price; Mr. Simon Bendall of Baldwin's, London; Herr Hans von Aulock, Istanbul; Mr. J. Mossop, Holbeach, Spalding, Lincolnshire, England; the Hunterian Collection, Glasgow; the Magyar Nemzeti Muzeum, Budapest; the State Hermitage, Leningrad; the American Numismatic Society New York, and particularly Dr. Margaret Thomson; the Museum of Fine Arts, Boston; to the Museum of Art and Archaeology of the University of Missouri, Columbia; to Mr. Hans-Jörg Bloesch, Winterthur; Dr. R. Göbl, Vienna; the staff of E. J. Brill; and to many others too numerous to mention who have helped with advice and information.

For permission to reproduce photographs I should thank the Royal Collection of Coins and Medals, Copenhagen; the Staatliche Museen, Preussischer Kulturbesitz; the Deutsches Archäologisches Institut, Abteiling Istanbul; the Indiana University Art Museum, Bloomington; Manchester University Press and the Österreichische Akademie der Wissenschaften.

Last but not least, particular thanks go to my student, Mr. Carl Berkowitz, who with his indefatigable gathering of material for me spared me the necessity of trips to such places as Brussels, Adana, and Jerusalem; and to Ann Wright, our secretary here in Columbia, for her help as a typist. Thanks for financial support go to the American Philosophical Society, the American Council of Learned Societies, the Research Council of the University of Missouri, and the University of Missouri-Columbia Alumni Development Fund.

Columbia, Missouri   EUGENE N. LANE

BIBLIOGRAPHICAL ABBREVIATIONS

All works referred to more than once or twice in the text of this volume are referred to by abbreviations, a table of which is given below:

Annuario	*Annuario della Scuola Archeologica di Atene*, Bergamo, etc., 1914-
BCH	*Bulletin de Correspondance Hellenique*, Paris, 1877-
BMC Caria	*British Museum Catalogue of Greek Coins, Caria and Islands*, London, 1897 (by B. F. Head)
BMC Ionia	*British Museum Catalogue of Greek Coins, Ionia*, London, 1892 (by B. F. Head)
BMC Galatia	*British Museum Catalogue of Greek Coins, Galatia, Cappadocia, and Syria*, London, 1899 (by W. Wroth)
BMC Lycia	*British Museum Catalogue of Greek Coins, Lycia, Pamphylia, and Pisidia*, London, 1897 (by G. F. Hill)
BMC Lycaonia	*British Meseum Catalogue of Greek Coins, Lycaonia, Isauria, and Cilicia*, London, 1900 (by G. F. Hill)
BMC Lydia	*British Museum Catalogue of Greek Coins, Lydia*, London, 1901, (by B. F. Head)
BMC Phrygia	*British Museum Catalogue of Greek Coins, Phrygia*, London, 1906 (by B. F. Head)
BCH Pontus	*British Museum Catalogue of Greek Coins, Pontus, Paphlagonia, Bithynia and Bosporus* (by W. Wroth), London, 1899
Drexler	W. Drexler, article, s.v. Men in W. H. Roscher's *Lexikon des Griechischen und Römischen Mythologie*, Leipzig, ca. 1896
Fiorelli	Fiorelli, *Medagliere di Napoli*, Naples, 1867-71
Grose	S. W. Grose, *Fitzwilliam Museum, MacLean Collection*, Cambridge, 1923-29
Hübl	A. Hübl, *Die Münzsammlung des Stiftes Schotten*, Vienna, 1910-1920
Hunt.	G. MacDonald, *Hunterian Collection, Greek Coins*, Glasgow, 1899-1905
Imhoof, Gr. M.	F. Imhoof-Blumer, *Griechische Münzen* (Akademie der Wissenschaften, München, Philosophisch-Philologische Klasse, Abhandlungen, XVIII, 3), Munich, 1890
Imhoof, Kl. M.	F. Imhoof-Blumer, *Kleinasiatische Münzen* (Sonderschrift des österreichischen archäologischen Instituts, 1 and 3), Vienna, 1900-1902
Imhoof, M. G.	F. Imhoof-Blumer, *Monnaies Grecques* (Akademie van Wetenschappen, Amsterdam, Verhandelingen, Afdeling Letterkunde, 14), Amsterdam, 1883

Inv. Wadd.	E. Babelon, *Inventaire Sommaire de la Collection Waddington*, in *Revue Numismatique*, 1897-98
JIAN	*Journal International d'Archéologie Numismatique*, Athens, 1898-1927
JNuG	*Jahrbuch für Numismatik und Geldgeschichte*, Munich, etc., 1949-
Kraft	Konrad Kraft, *Das System der kaiserzeitlichen Münzprägung in Kleinasien* (Istanbuler Forschungen, 29) Berlin, 1972
Krzyzanowska, MC	Aleksandra Krzyzanowska, *Monnaies Coloniales d'Antioche de Pisidie* (Travaux du centre d'archéologie méditeranéenne de l'académie polonaise des sciences, 7), Warsaw, 1970
Lane II	E. N. Lane, "A Restudy of the God Men, II," *Berytus*, XVII, 1967, pp. 13-47
Lane III	E. N. Lane, "A Re-Study of the God Men, III," *Berytus*, XVII, 1968, pp. 81-106
Metzger	H. Metzger, *Catalogue des monuments votifs du musée d'Adalia* (Etudes orientales, 11), Paris, 1952
Mionnet	T. Mionnet, *Description de médailles antiques*, Paris, 1809-37
NC	*Numismatic Chronicle*, London, 1838-
NS	*Numizmaticheskiy Sbornik*, Moscow, 1911-15
NZ	*Numismatische Zeitschrift*, Vienna, 1870-1949
Niggeler	*Sammlung Walter Niggeler* (Auction catalogue), Zürich and Basel, 1966
RBN	*Revue Belge de Numismatique*, Brussels, 1898-
RN	*Revue Numismatique*, Paris, 1856-
Recueil	W. H. Waddington, E. Babelon, and Th. Reinach, *Recueil Général des Monnaies Grecques d'Asie Mineure*, Paris, 1904-12
Regling, Nysa	K. Regling, "Ein Überblick über die Münzprägung von Nysa," in *Nysa ad Mäandrum* (Jahrbuch des Deutschen Archäologischen Instituts, Ergänzungsheft, 10, 1913, pp. 70-103)
Regling, Priene	K. Regling, *Die Münzen von Priene*, Berlin, 1927
Roscher	W. H. Roscher, Über die Reiterstatue Iul. Caesars auf dem Forum Iulium und den ἵππος βροτόπους einer Münze des Gordianus Pius von Nikaia (Bithynien). (Sächsische Akademie der Wissenschaften, Berichte, Philologisch-Historische Klasse, 43, 1891, pp. 96 ff.).
SNG Aulock	*Sylloge Nummorum Graecorum, Deutschland, Sammlung von Aulock*, Berlin, 1957-
SNG Cop., Caria	*Sylloge Nummorum Graecorum, Danish National Museum, Caria*, Copenhagen, 1947
SNG Cop., Cyprus	etc., Copenhagen, 1956
SNG Cop., Ionia	*Sylloge Nummorum Graeocorum, Danish National Museum, Ionia*, Copenhagen, 1946

SNG Cop., Lycia   *Sylloge Nummorum Graecorum, Danish National Museum, Lycia-Pamphylia*, Copenhagen, 1955
SNG Cop., Lydia   *Sylloge Nummorum Graecorum, Danish National Museum, Lydia*, Copenhagen, 1947
SNG Cop., Lycaonia   *Sylloge Nummorum Graecorum, Danish National Museum, Lycaonia-Cilicia*, Copenhagen, 1956
SNG Cop., Pisidia   *Sylloge Nummorum Graecorum, Danish National Museum, Pisidia*, Copenhagen, 1956
SNG Cop., Phrygia   *Sylloge Nummorum Graecorum, Danish National Museum, Phrygia*, Copenhagen, 1948
SNG Cop., Syria: Cities *Sylloge Nummorum Graecorum, Danish Museum, Syria: Cities*, Copenhagen, 1959
SNG Fitz.   *Sylloge Nummorum Graecorum, Great Britain, IV, Fitzwilliam Museum, Leake and General Collections*
SNR   *Schweizerische Numismatische Rundschau*, Geneva, 1891-
Torino, Monete Grece   *Regio Museo Torino, Monete Greece*, 1883
WN   *Wiadmosci Numizmatyczne*, Warsaw, 1957-
Weber   L. Forrer, *The Weber Collection*, London, 1922-29
Z. für N.   *Zeitschrift für Numismatik*, Berlin, 1874-1935

COINS

Pharnaceia 1   Plate I

Obv.: Bust of Men, r., with laurel wreath on cap
No inscription
Rev.: Eight-pointed star, with the inscription Φαρνακέων counter-clockwise around the outside

> Bibliography:
> Imhoof, *Kl. M.*, I, p. 5, Pharnakeia 1 and Pl. I, no. 3
> *Recueil*, I, 1², p. 138, no. 1 and Pl. XIV, 15
> Lane II, p. 14, no. 1

Weight: 5.52 gr. (Berlin)
Illustrated example: Berlin
Remarks: Generally dated to the second century B.C., before the time of Mithadates Eupator.

Gangra-Germanicopolis 1   Plate I

Obv.: Bust of Julia Domna, r.
Inscription: Ἰουλ. Δόμνα Σεβαστ.
Rev.: Men sitting on a stool, facing l. In his l. hand he holds a staff, in his r., a patera.
Inscription: Γερμανικοπόλεως θεῶν ἑστίας

> Bibliography:
> Drexler, col. 2692
> *Recueil*, I, 1², p. 192, no. 36, and Pl. XXII, no. 25
> *SNG Fitz.*, Pl. 74, no. 4065
> Lane, II, p. 15, note 5: III, p. 104, no. 1

Weight: 14.32 gr. (Cambridge)
Illustrated example: Paris

Bithynium-Claudiopolis 1   Plate I

Obv.: Bust of Elagabalus, r.
Inscription: M. Αὐρη. Ἀντωνῖνος Αὐγου.
Rev.: Men standing slightly l., head r., holding scepter in r. hand
Inscription: Βιθυνιέων Ἀδριανῶν

Bibliography:
Inv. Wadd., RN, 1897, p. 286, no. 245
Recueil, I, 2, p. 276, no. 54, and Pl. XLIII, no. 7
Lane, II, p. 15, Bithynium 1

Weight: 9.60 gr. (Paris)
Illustrated example: Paris

Juliopolis 1   Plate I

Obv.: Bust of Commodus, r., laureate
Inscription: A.K.Λ. Αἰλ. Κομ. Ἡρακλῆς Ῥωμ.
Rev.: Bust of Men, r., cap ornamented with stars, apparently wearing earrings
Inscription: Ἰουλιοπολειτῶν

Bibliography:
Roscher, p. 141, and Pl. Ia, no. 1
Drexler, col. 2692
BMC Pontus, p. 149, Juliopolis 2, and Pl. XXXI, no. 5 (rev. only)
Recueil, I, 2, p. 385, no. 5 and Pl. LXIII, 5
SNG Aulock, Pl. 240, no. 6970
Lane, II, p. 15, Juliopolis 1: III, p. 103, no. 13
Niggeler, II, no. 590

Weight: 8.63 gr. (Aulock) - 14.28 gr. (Niggeler)
Illustrated example: Niggeler

Juliopolis 2   Plate I

Obv.: Bust of Commodus, r., laureate
Inscription: Α. Κ. Λ. Αἰλ. Αὐρ. Κομ. Ἡρακλῆς Ῥωμ.
Rev.: Men riding r.
Inscription: Ἰουλιοπολειτῶν

Bibliography:
Drexler, col. 2693
Inv. Wadd., RN, 1897, p. 292, no. 374
Recueil, I, 2, p. 386, no. 6 and Pl. LXIII, no. 6 (rev. only)
SNG Aulock, Pl. 240, no. 6969
Lane, II, p. 16, Juliopolis 11: III, p. 103, no. 12

Weight: 8.83 gr. (Paris) - 11.34 gr. (Aulock)
Illustrated example: Aulock

Juliopolis 3 Plate I

Obv.: Bust of Julia Domna, r.
Inscription: Ἰουλία Σεβαστή
Rev.: Men riding r.
Inscription: Ἰουλιοπολειτῶν

> Bibliography:
> Drexler, col. 2693
> *Recueil*, I, 2, p. 387, no. 20

Weight: 8.53 gr. (Vienna)
Illustrated example: Vienna

Juliopolis 4 Plate I

Obv.: Bust of Septimius Severus, r., laureate
Inscription: Αὐ. Κ. Λ. Σεπτ. Σευῆρος Π. Σ.
Rev.: Bust of Men, stars on cap
Inscription: Ἰουλιοπολειτῶν

> Bibliography:
> Josef Scholz, *NZ*, 1901, p. 32, no. 43 and Pl. VI (rev. only)
> *Recueil*, I, 2, p. 386, no. 11 and Pl. LXIII, no. 10
> Lane, II, p. 15, Juliopolis 2

Weight: 8.55 gr. (Scholz)
Illustrated example: Berlin

Juliopolis 5 Plate I

Obv.: Bust of Septimius Severus, r., laureate
Inscription: Αὐ. Λ. Σεπτι. Σεουῆρος Πε.
Rev.: Men riding r., turning head back, extending r. hand with stick-like attribute
Inscription: Ἰουλιοπολειτῶν

> Bibliography:
> Imhoof-Blumer, *SNR*, 1904, p. 192-3, Juliopolis 1

Weight: 12.50 gr. (Berlin)
Illustrated example: Berlin
Remarks: It is questionable whether Men is actually intended.

Juliopolis 6 Plate I

Obv.: Bust of young Caracalla, r., laureate
Inscription: Ἀντωνῖνος Αὐγ.
Rev.: Bust of Men with starry cap. Very womanish appearance.
Inscription: Ἰουλιοπολειτῶν

> Bibliography:
> Roscher, p. 147
> W. M. Ramsay, *Cities and Bishoprics of Phrygia*, Oxford, 1895, I, p. 54
> Drexler, col. 2692
> *Recueil*, I, 2, p. 388, no. 26, and Pl. LXIII, 21
> Lane, II, p. 15, Juliopolis 3

Weight: 12.03 gr. (Vienna) - 14.42 gr. (Paris)
Illustrated example: Paris

Juliopolis 7 Plate I

Obv.: Bust of Caracalla, r., as Augustus
Inscription: Μ. Αὐρ. Ἀντωνῖνος Κ.
Rev.: Bust of Men, r., stars on cap
Inscription: Ἰουλιοπολειτῶν

> Bibliography:
> *Recueil*, I, 2, p. 388, no. 26 bis
> Münsterberg, *NZ*, 54, 1921, p. 135

Weight: 11.46 gr. (Vienna)
Illustrated example: Vienna

Juliopolis 8 Plate II

Obv.: Bust of young Caracalla, r., laureate, as Augustus
Inscription: Ἀντωνῖνος Αὐγ.
Rev.: Men riding r.
Inscription: Ἰουλιοπολειτῶν

> Bibliography:
> R. Münsterberg, *NZ*, 54, 1921, p. 135

Weight: 10.54 gr. (Vienna)
Illustrated example: Vienna

COINS 5

Juliopolis 9 Plate II

Obv.: Bust of Caracalla, r., bearded, laureate
Inscription: Αὐτ. Κ. 'Αντωνῖνος Αὐγ.
Rev.: Men standing l. with patera over altar
Inscription: 'Ιουλιοπολειτῶν

    Bibliography: none

Weight: unavailable
Illustrated example: Adana

Juliopolis 10 Plate II

Obv.: Bust of Severus Alexander, r., laureate
Inscription: Μ. Αὐρ. Σευ. 'Αλέξανδρος Αὐγ.
Rev.: Bust of Men, r., with starry cap
Inscription: 'Ιουλιοπολειτῶν

    Bibliography:
    Drexler, col. 2693
    Recueil, I, 2, p. 391, no. 42 and Pl. LXIV, 11
    Lane, II, p. 15, Juliopolis 4

Weight: 9.84 gr. (Paris)
Illustrated example: Paris

Juliopolis 11 Plate II

Obv.: Bust of Maximinus, r., laureate
Inscription: Γ. 'Ιου. Οὐη. Μαξιμεῖνος Αὐγ.
Rev.: Men standing l. with scepter in l. hand, pine-cone in r.
Inscription: 'Ιουλιοπολειτῶν

    Bibliography:
    Drexler, col. 2693
    BMC Pontus, p. 151, no. 10 and Pl. XXXI, no. 9 (rev. only)
    Recueil, I, 2, p. 391, no. 47 and Pl. LXIV, 15
    Lane, II, p. 15, Juliopolis 6

Weight: 3.03 gr. (London) - 3.14 (Vienna)
Illustrated example: London

Juliopolis 12 Plate II

Obv.: Bust of Maximinus, r., laureate
Inscription: Γ. 'Ιου. Ούη Μαξιμεῖνος Αὐγ.
Rev.: Men standing l., holding patera over altar in r. hand, staff in l.
Inscription: 'Ιουλιοπολειτῶν

> Bibliography:
> *SNG Aulock*, Pl. 240, no. 6974
> Lane, III, p. 103, no. 14

Weight: 6.83 gr. (Aulock)
Illustrated example: Aulock

Juliopolis 13 Plate II

Obv.: Bust of Maximus, r., bareheaded
Inscription: Γ. 'Ιου. Ούη. Μάξιμος Κ.
Rev.: Men standing with staff in l. hand, patera over altar in r.
Inscription: 'Ιουλιοπολειτῶν

> Bibliography:
> Drexler, col. 2693
> *Recueil*, I, 2, p. 392, no. 51 and Pl. LXIV, 19
> Lane, II, p. 15, Juliopolis 7

Weight: 6.45 gr. (Berlin)
Illustrated example: Berlin

Juliopolis 14 Plate II

Obv.: Bust of Gordian III, r., laureate
Inscription: Μ. 'Αντ. Γορδιανὸς Αὐ.
Rev.: Bust of Men, r., with starry cap
Inscription: 'Ιουλιοπολειτῶν

> Bibliography:
> Lane, II, p. 15, Juliopolis 5 and Pl. III, no. 1

Weight: 8.16 gr. (Gotha)
Illustrated example: Gotha

Juliopolis 15   Plate II

Obv.: Bust of Philip I, r., radiate
Inscription: M. 'Ιούλιος Φίλιππος Αύγ.
Rev.: Men standing l., patera in r. hand, staff in l.
Inscription: 'Ιουλιοπολειτῶν

> Bibliography:
> *SNG Aulock*, Pl. 15, no. 474
> Lane, II, P. 16, Juliopolis 8

Weight: 11.57 gr. (Aulock)
Illustrated example: Aulock

Juliopolis 16   Plate II

Obv.: Bust of Valerian, r., radiate
Inscription: Που. Λικ. Ούαλεριανὸς Σεβ.
Rev.: Men standing l., holding patera in r. hand, staff in l.
Inscription: 'Ιουλιοπολειτῶν

> Bibliography:
> Theodor Prowe, *Aus Meiner Sammlung* (NS, I, 1911) p. 332, no. 10, and Pl. XVI, 10
> *SNG Aulock*, Pl. 15, no. 476
> Lane, II, p. 16, Juliopolis 9
> Kraft, Pl. 106, no. 0

Weight: 7.07 gr. (Aulock)
Illustrated example: Aulock

Juliopolis 17   Plate II

Obv.: Bust of Gallienus, r., radiate
Inscription: Πο. Λι. 'Εγν. Γαλλιηνὸς Σεβ.
Rev.: Men standing l. with patera in r. hand, staff in l.
Inscription: 'Ιουλιοπολειτῶν

> Bibliography:
> Drexler, col. 2693
> *BMC Pontus*, Juliopolis 13
> *Recueil*, I, 2, p. 393, no. 59 and Pl. LXIV, 25 (rev. only)
> Lane, II, p. 16, Juliopolis 10
> Drexler, col. 2693

Weight: 8.10 gr. (Istanbul)
Illustrated example: Istanbul

Elaia Aeolidis 1   Plate III

Obv.: Bust of Gordian r., r.
Inscription: Αὐτο. Κ. Μ. ᾿Αντ. Γορδιανός
Rev.: Men standing l., holding staff in l. hand and pine-cone in r.
Inscription: ᾿Επὶ Σεβήρου ᾿Ελαειτῶν

> Bibliography:
> Drexler, col. 2696-7
> Lane, II, p. 16, Elaea 1 and Pl. III, 2 (rev. only)

Weight: 4.61gr. - 6.29 gr. (Berlin)
Illustrated example: Berlin

Elaia 2   Plate III

Obv.: Bust of Senate, r.
Inscription: ῾Ιερὰ Σύγκλητος
Rev.: Men standing l. with pine-cone and staff
Inscription: ᾿Επὶ Σεβήρου ᾿Ελαειτῶν

> Bibliography: none

Weight: 3.57 gr. (Athens)
Illustrated example: Athens

Magnesia on the Maeander 1   Plate III

Obv.: Bust of Caracalla, r., laureate
Inscription: Μ. Αὐρ. ᾿Αντωνεῖνος
Rev.: Men standing frontally with thyrsus (spear?) in r. hand, torch held downward in his l. To his l., a thyrsus entwined by a snake.
Inscription: ᾿Επὶ γρ. Φλ. Βάσσου Μαγνητῶν

> Bibliography:
> Drexler, Z. für N., 1887, pp. 77-78
> Roscher, p. 128c, p. 144 and Pl. IV, no. 1 (rev. only)
> Drexler, col. 2797
> Lane, II, p. 16 Magnesia 4

Weight: 15.82 gr. (Paris)
Illustrated example: Paris

Magnesia 2 Plate III

Obv.: Bust of Julia Domna, r.
Inscription: ’Ιουλία Δόμνα Σεβ.
Rev.: Men as on preceding coin
Inscription: ’Επὶ γρ. Φλ. Β'ασσου Μαγνητῶν

> Bibliography:
> Imhoof-Blumer, *Kl. M.*, p. 81, no. 32

Weight: 13.52 (Berlin)
Illustrated example: Berlin

Magnesia 3 Plate III

Obv.: Bust of Julia Mamaea, r.
Inscription: ’Ιουλία Μαμαῖα Σεβ.
Rev.: Men standing frontally, with thyrsus (spear?) in his l. hand, a patera (torch?) held downward in his r. hand, and thyrsus with snakes (ribbons?) in the field to his r.
Inscription: ’Επὶ γρα. Φωτεινοῦ Μαγνητῶν

> Bibliography:
> Sabatier, *RBN*, 1863, p. 148 and Pl. XII, no. 14
> Drexler, *Z. für N.*, 15, p. 76
> Roscher, pp. 127-8, a
> Drexler, col. 2697
> *Inv. Wadd.*, *RN*, 1897, p. 366, no. 1750
> *SNG Fitz.*, Pl. 87, no. 4522

Weight: 10.00 gr. (Cambridge) - 11.09 (Paris)
Illustrated example: Cambridge

Magnesia 4 Plate III

Obv.: Bust of Julia Mamaea, r.
Inscription: ’Ιουλία Μαμαῖα Σεβ.
Rev.: Men as on Magnesia 1 and 2, left-right reversed from Magnesia 3
Inscription: Μαγνητῶν νεωκόρων τῆς ’Αρτέμιδος

> Bibliography:
> Drexler, p. 128b; p. 144, Pl. Ib, no. 2 (rev. only)

Drexler, *Z. für N.*, 15, p. 77
Drexler, col. 2697

Weight: 11.12 gr. (Paris)
Illustrated example: Paris

Magnesia 5 Plate III

Obv.: Bust of Maximinus, r., laureate
Inscription: Αὐτ. Κ. Γ. Οὐη. Μαξιμεῖνος
Rev.: Men standing l., in r. hand pine-cone, in l. staff. In field, star.
Inscription: Μαγνητῶν

>Bibliography:
>Drexler, col. 2697
>*BMC Ionia*, p. 169, no. 77
>Lane, II, p. 16, Magnesia 1, and Pl. III, 3

Weight: 4.83 gr. (London)
Illustrated example: London

Magnesia 6 Plate III

Obv.: Bust of Maximinus r., laureate
Inscription: Αὐτ. Κ. Γ. Οὐη. Μαξιμεῖνος
Rev.: Men standing l., holding patera over flaming altar, staff in l. hand
Inscription: Ἐπὶ γρ. Τυχικοῦ Μαγνητῶν

>Bibliography:
>Rayet and Thomas, *Milet et le Golfe Latmique*, Paris, 1877, p. 128, fig. 29
>Drexler, col. 2697
>Lane, II, p. 16, Magnesia 3 and Pl. III, 4

Weight: 8.23 gr. (Paris)
Illustrated example: (Paris)

Magnesia 7 Plate III

Obv.: Bust of Maximus, r., laureate
Inscription: Γι. Οὐη. Μάξιμος Καῖσαρ (with variations)

Rev.: Men standing l., pine-cone in r. hand, staff in l. In field, star.
Inscription: Μαγνητῶν

> Bibliography:
> Drexler, col. 2697
> *BMC Ionia*, p. 170, no. 80 and Pl. 20, no. 5 (rev. only)
> Weber, III, i, p. 269, no. 6016
> Lane, II, p. 16, Magnesia 2

Weight: 3.37 (Weber) - 4.45 gr. (London)
Illustrated example: Weber

Magnesia 8   Plate III

Obv.: Bust of Maximus, r., laureate
Inscription: Γι. Οὐη. Μάξιμος
Rev.: Men standing r., with staff in l., holding a patera(?) over an altar (?)
Inscription: Μαγνητῶν

> Bibliography:
> *SNG Cop., Ionia*, Pl. 20, no. 891

Weight: 4.62 gr. (Copenhagen)
Illustrated example: Copenhagen

Magnesia 9   Plate IV

Obv.: Bust of Philip I, r., laureate
Inscription: Αὐτ. Κ. Μ. ’Ιου. Φίλιππος
Rev.: Men standing l. with patera and staff, bucranium at feet
Inscription: ’Επὶ γρ. Φλ. Περιγένους Μαγνητῶν

> Bibliography: none

Weight: 18.56 gr. (London)
Illustrated example: London

Priene 1   Plate IV

Obv.: Bust of the philosopher Bias, r.
Inscription: Βίας counterclockwise

Rev.: Men standing l. with patera in r. hand, scepter in l.
Inscription: Πριηνέων counterclockwise

> Bibliography:
> A. de Longperier, *RN*, 1869-70, p. 378
> Imhoof, *Kl. M.*, I, p. 94, no. 4
> Regling, *Priene*, no. 185, and Pl. IV
> Lane, II, p. 17, Priene 1

Weight: 1.71 gr. - 3.01 gr. (examples known to Regling)
Illustrated example: Berlin

Priene 2   Plate IV

Obv.: Bust of the philosopher Bias, r.
Inscription: Βίας clockwise
Rev.: Men standing l., patera in r. hand, staff in l.
Inscription: Πριηνέων clockwise

> Bibliography:
> Imhoof, *Kl. M.*, I, p. 94, no. 5 and Pl. III, no. 22
> Regling, *Priene*, no. 184, and Pl. IV

Weight: 3.44 gr. - 5.10 gr. (examples known to Regling)
Illustrated example: Berlin (composite of two examples)

Priene 3   Plate IV

Obv.: Bust of Maximus, r., laureate
Inscription: Γ. ’Ι. Οὐη. Μάξιμος
Rev.: Men standing l., with patera in r. hand, staff in l.
Inscription: Πριηνέων

> Bibliography:
> Imhoof, *Kl. M.*, I, p. 95, no. 8
> Regling, *Priene*, no. 214 and Pl. V
> Lane, II, p. 17, Priene 2

Weight: 4.32 gr. (Berlin)
Illustrated example: Berlin

Priene 4   Plate IV

Obv.:   Bust of Otacilia Severa, r.
Inscription: M. 'Ωτα. Σευῆρα Σεβα.
Rev.:   Men standing l., patera in r. hand, staff in l.
Inscription: 'Επὶ ἀρχιπρυ. Μοσχίωνος Πριηνέων

> Bibliography:
> Roscher, col. 2697
> *BMC Ionia*, p. 235, no. 56
> Regling, *Priene*, no. 215, and Pl. V
> Lane, II, p. 17, Priene 3
> Kraft, Pl. XV, no. 112

Weight: 9.18 gr.-10.99 gr. (examples known to Regling)
Illustrated example: London

Priene 5   Plate IV

Obv.:   Bust of Herennius Etruscus, l., bareheaded
Inscription: Νου. Του. Η. Μω. Λτητου. Με. Τρλ. counterclockwise
Rev.:   Men standing l. with patera in r. hand, staff in l.
Inscription: 'Επὶ ἀρ. Εὐτύχηδος Πριηνέων counterclockwise, with variations

> Bibliography:
> Imhoof, *MG*, p. 468, no. 55
> *Inv. Wadd.*, *RN*, 1898, p. 56, no. 3779
> Imhoof, *Kl. M.*, p. 95, no. 9
> Regling, *Priene*, nos. 217-218, and Pl. V
> Lane, II, p. 17, Priene 4; p. 34, Pappa-Tiberia 2, and Pl. X, no. 1

Weight: 8.98 gr.-11.37 gr. (examples known to Regling)
Illustrated example: Berlin
Remarks: Originally attributed both by Imhoof and by Babelon to Pappa-Tiberia.

Priene 6   Plate IV

Obv.:   Bust of Valerian, r., laureate
Inscription: Αὐτ. Κ. Πο. Λικ. Οὐλεριανός
Rev.:   Men standing l., with staff in l. hand, patera in r.
Inscription: 'Επ' ἀρχ. 'Ιουλ. Σατορνείνου Πριηνέων

Bibliography:
Regling, *Priene*, no. 223, and Pl. V
Lane, II, p. 17, Priene 5

Weight: 9.25 gr. (Berlin)

Illustrated example: From Regling, a composite of Berlin rev., with a Copenhagen coin having same obv. die.

Remarks: Although crescent is lacking, identification as Men is probable, because of known Men-coins of Priene. The same situation exists at Sardis and at Hierapolis.

Priene 7   Plate IV

Obv.: Bust of Salonina, r.
Inscription: Σαλων. Χρυσογένης
Rev.: Men standing l., with patera in r. hand, staff in l.
Inscription: Ἐπ. ἀρχ. Γ. ᾽Ιουλ. Σατορνείνου Πριηνέων

Bibliography:
Imhoof, *Kl. M.*, I, p. 96, no. 11
Regling, *Priene*, p. 117, no. 228, and Pl. V
Kraft, Pl. XXV, no. 155b

Weight: 10.99 gr. (Berlin)
Illustrated example: Berlin

Bageis 1   Plate V

Obv.: Bust of Men, r., border of dots
Inscription: Καισαρέων counterclockwise
Rev.: Humped bull standing l., head turned to face viewer
Inscription: Βαγηνῶν counterclockwise

Bibliography:
Drexler, col. 2699
Imhoof-Blumer, *SNR*, VI, 1898, p. 198, no. 1
BMC Lydia, p. 30, and Pl. IV, no. 5
Inv. Wadd., *RN*. 1898, p. 344, no. 4883, and Pl. IX, 2
SNG Cop., *Lydia*, Pl. 2, no. 42
Lane, II, p. 17, Bageis 1

Weight: 2.51 gr. (Paris - 3.37 gr. (London)
Illustrated example: Copenhagen
Remarks: Berlin has a copy with reverse incuse, of which an illustration is given here, as a curiosity.

COINS   15

Bageis 2   Plate V

Obv.:   Bust of Men, r., border of dots
Inscription: Βαγηνῶν
Rev.:   Humped bull standing r., facing viewer.
Inscription: 'Επὶ 'Απολλοδώρου

   Bibliography:
   Imhoof, *Kl, M.*, I, p. 169, Bageis 1 and Pl. VI, 1 (Berlin)

Weight: 2.00 gr. (New York)
Illustrated example: Berlin

Bageis 3   Plate V

Alliance coin of Bageis and Temenothyrae
Obv.:   Bust of Gallienus r., laureate, with aegis
Inscription: Αὐ. Κα. Πο. Λικ. Γαλλιηνός
Rev.:   Men on l. of coin, with staff in r. hand, pine-cone in l.; Tyche on r. of coin, with kalathos, rudder and cornucopia; the two divinities face each other.
Inscription: Καισαρέων Βαγηνῶν Τημενοθυρέων ὁμόνοια (ὁμόνυα on some examples)

   Bibliography:
   Drexler, col. 2699
   BMC Lydia, p. 41, nos. 54-56 and Pl. XLI, no. 1 (rev. only)
   Weber, III, ii, p. 428, no. 6789
   SNG Cop., Lydia, Pl. 2, no. 58
   SNG Aulock, Pl. 93, no. 2918
   Niggeler, no. 624
   Lane, II, p. 17, Bageis 2

Weight: 19.88 gr. (London) - 35.12 (Weber)
Illustrated example: Aulock

Gordus-Julia 1   Plate V

Obv.:   Bust of the Senate, r.
Inscription: Ἱερὰ Σύγκλητος (various arrangements)
Rev.:   Men standing l. with patera in r. hand, staff in l.
Inscription: 'Ιουλιέων Γορδηνῶν

Bibliography:
Pierre de Saxe-Cobourg, *RN*, 1891, p. 4, no. 13 and Pl. II, no. 13
Drexler, col. 2700
BMC Lydia, Gordus-Julia 6
Lane, II, p. 18, Gordus-Julia 1 and Pl. III, no. 5

Weight: 3.96 gr. (Athens) - 4.91 gr. (London)
Illustrated example: Athens

Gordus-Julia 2   Plate V

Obv.:   Bust of Trajan, r., laureate
Inscription: Τραιανὸς Σεβ. Γερ. Δακικός
Rev.:   Men standing l., pine-cone in r. hand, staff in l., lions at feet
Inscription: ʼΕπὶ Ποπλίου Γορδηνῶν

Bibliography:
Imhoof, *Kl. M.*, I, p. 172, no. 3 and Pl. VI, no. 3
Lane, II, p. 18, Gordus-Julia 2

Weight: 8.92 gr. (Istanbul)
Illustrated example: Istanbul

Gordus-Julia 3   Plate V

Obv.:   Bust of Trajan, r., laureate
Inscription: Τραιανὸς Σεβ. Γερ. Δακικός
Rev.:   Men standing l., patera in r. hand, staff in l.
Inscription: Γορδηνῶν ʼΙουλιέων Π Ρ

Bibliography:
Inv. Wadd., *RN*, 1898, p. 351, no. 4974

Weight: 4.36 gr. (Paris)
Illustrated example: Paris

Gordus-Julia 4   Plate V

Obv.:   Bust of Lucius Verus, r., laureate
Inscription: Αὐτ. Και. Λ. Αὐρη. Οὐῆρος
Rev.:   Men standing l. with patera and staff
Inscription: ʼΕπὶ ʼΙουλιανοῦ ʼΙουλιέων Γορδηνῶν

Bibliography: none

Weight: 10.55 gr. (Paris)
Illustrated example: Paris

Gordus-Julia 5   Plate V

Obv.: Bust of Commodus, r., youthful, laureate
Inscription: Αὐ Λ. Αὐρ. Κόμοδος
Rev.: Men standing l., with patera in r. hand, staff in l., lions at feet
Inscription: 'Ιουλιέων Γορδηνῶν

> Bibliography:
> W. H. Scott, *NC*, 1851-52, p. 120
> Drexler, col. 2700
> *BMC Lydia*, p. 95, nos. 31-32 and Pl. X, 5
> *Inv. Wadd.*, *RN*, 1898, p. 351, no. 4977
> *SNG Cop.*, *Lydia*, Pl. 5, no. 160
> Lane, II, p. 18, Gordus-Julia 3

Weight: 9.21 gr. (Cop.) - 12.21 gr. (London)
Illustrated example: Copenhagen

Gordus-Julia 6   Plate V

Obv.: Bust of Septimius Severus, r., laureate
Inscription: Αὐτ. Καισ. Λ. Σεπτι. Σεουῆρος Περ.
Rev.: Men standing l., with patera in r. hand, staff in l., lions at feet, facing away from him
Inscription: 'Επὶ 'Ιουλίου Μαρ. ἀρχ. α' τὸ β' 'Ιουλιέων Γορδηνῶν

> Bibliography:
> P. Clemens Sibilian, *NZ*, 1870, p. 320
> Drexler, col. 2700
> *SNG Aulock*, Pl. 95, no. 2985
> Lane, II, p. 18, Gordus-Julia 4

Weight: 19.22 gr. (Vienna) - 20.13 gr. (Aulock)
Illustrated example: Aulock

Gordus-Julia 7   Plate VI

Obv.: Bust of Septimius Severus, r., laureate
Inscription: Αὐ Και. Λ. Επ. Σεουῆρος Περ.

Rev.: Men standing l. with patera in r. hand, staff in l., lions at feet
Inscription: 'Ιουλιέων Γορδηνῶν

> Bibliography:
> Kraft, Pl. 69, no. 50b

Weight: 9.59 (Berlin-pierced)
Illustrated example: Berlin

Gordus-Julia 8   Plate VI

Obv.: Bust of Macrinus, r., laureate
Inscription: Αὐτ. Κ. Μ. 'Οπελ. Σεου. Μακρεῖνος
Rev.: Men standing l. with pine-cone and staff, lions at feet
Inscription: 'Επ. Αἰλ. Ζωσίμου ἀρχ. α' τὸ β' 'Ιουλιέω. Γορδηνῶν

> Bibliography:
> BMC Lydia, p. 97, Gordus-Julia 41

Weight: 24.17 gr. (London)
Illustrated example: London

Maeonia 1   Plate VI

Obv.: Bust of Nero, r., laureate
Inscription: Νέρων Καῖσαρ counterclockwise
Rev.: Men standing l., pine-cone in r. hand, staff in l.
Inscription: 'Επ. Τι. Κλ. Μενεκράτους Μαιονῶν counterclockwise

> Bibliography:
> Drexler, col. 2700
> BMC Lydia, p. 131, no. 35, and Pl. XIV, no. 4 (rev. only)
> Inv. Wadd., RN, 1898, p. 356, no. 5061
> Lane, II, p. 18, Maeonia 1

Weight: 2.49 gr.-3.17 gr. (Paris)
Illustrated example: Paris

Maeonia 2   Plate VI

Obv.: Bust of Nero, r., laureate
Inscription: Νέρων Καῖσαρ
Rev.: Bust of Men, r.
Inscription: 'Επ. Μενεκράτους Μαιονῶν

Bibliography:
BMC Lydia, p. 132, no. 36 and Pl. XIV, 5 (rev. only)
Lane, II, p. 18, Maeonia 2

Weight: 2.79 gr. (London)
Illustrated example: London

Nysa 1   Plate VI

Obv.: Bust of Men, r.
No inscription
Rev.: The word Νυσαέων within a wreath. There exist variations in letter-forms.

Bibliography:
Regling, *Nysa*, p. 78, no. 41 and Pl. XII
Lane, II, p. 18, Nysa 1

Weight: 3.39 gr. (Paris) - 4.72 gr. (Vienna)
Illustrated example: Berlin

Nysa 2   Plate VI

Obv.: Bust of Nero, r., as Caesar
Inscription: Νέρων Καῖσαρ counterclockwise
Rev.: Bust of Men, r.
Inscription: Νυσαέων counterclockwise
Variations exist in letter forms.

Bibliography:
Drexler, col. 2705
BMC Lydia, Nysa 29, and Pl. XX, no. 3
Inv. Wadd., *RN*, 1897, p. 439, no. 2498
Regling, *Nysa*, p. 80, no. 62
SNG Cop., *Lydia*, Pl. X, nos. 312-313
Lane, II, p. 18, Nysa 2

Weight: 3.54 gr. (London) - 4.31 (Paris)
Illustrated example: Copenhagen

Nysa 3   Plate VI

Obv.: Bust of Nero, r., as Caesar
Inscription: Νέρων Καῖσαρ counterclockwise

Rev.: Men standing l., with patera in r. hand, staff in l.
Inscription: Δομετιανὸς Νυσαέων ἱερεύς counterclockwise and vertically

> Bibliography:
> Imhoof, *MG*, p. 313, no. 72a
> Drexler, col. 2705
> Regling, *Nysa*, p. 80, no. 58
> Lane, II, p. 18, Nysa 3 and Pl. III, 6

Weight: 12.67 gr. (London) - 13.32 gr. (Berlin)
Illustrated example: Berlin

Nysa 4 Plate VI

Obv.: Bust of Antoninus Pius, r., laureate
Inscription: Αὐτοκράτωρ Καῖσαρ 'Αδριαν. 'Αντωνεῖνος
Rev.: Men standing l. with patera in r. hand, staff in l.
Inscription: Καμαρείτης Νυσαέων

> Bibliography:
> Drexler, col. 2706
> Regling, *Nysa*, p. 81, nos. 70 and 74
> *SNG Fitz.*, Pl. 95, no. 4868
> Lane, II, Nysa 4 and Pl. III, no. 7, III, p. 104, no. 4

Weight: 14.63 gr. (Paris) - 20.71 gr. (Naples)
Illustrated examples: Paris and Cambridge
Remarks: Regling attributes the Paris and Naples examples to Hadrian, but they turn out on examination to belong to Antoninus Pius. I illustrate both Paris and Cambridge examples to prove the identity.

Nysa 5 Plate VII

Obv.: Bust of Marcus Aurelius, as Caesar, bareheaded
Inscription: Μ. Αὐρήλιος Οὐῆρος Καῖσαρ
Rev.: Men standing l., patera in r. hand, staff in l.
Inscription: Καμαρείτης Νυσαέων

> Bibliography:
> Drexler, col. 2706
> *BMC Lydia*, p. 177, no. 36
> Regling, *Nysa*, p. 81, no. 79
> Lane, II, p. 19, no. 5, and Pl. III, no. 8

Weight: 15.43 gr. (London)
Illustrated example: London

Nysa 6 Plate VII

Obv.: Bust of Marcus Aurelius, as Caesar, bareheaded
Inscription: Μ. Αὐρήλιος Οὖηρος Καῖσαρ
Rev.: Men standing l., with pine-cone in r. hand, staff in l., lions at feet
Inscription: Καμαρείτης Νυσαέων (?)

> Bibliography:
> Drexler, col. 2706
> Regling, *Nysa*, p. 81 bottom

Weight: 8.19 gr. (Berlin)
Illustrated example: Berlin
Remarks: This may have to be reattributed to Gordus-Iulia.

Nysa 7 Plate VII

Obv.: Bust of Marcus Aurelius, r., as Augustus, laureate
Inscription: 'Α. Κ. Μ. Α'υρ. 'Αντωνεῖνος Σεβ.
Rev.: Men standing l., with patera in r. hand, staff in l.
Inscription: 'Επ. γρ. 'Ασιατικοῦ Νυσαέων

> Bibliography:
> Drexler, col. 2705
> Regling, *Nysa*, p. 82, no. 85
> Lane, II, p. 19, no. 6, and Pl. III, no. 9

Weight: 17.92 gr. (Vienna)
Illustrated example: Vienna

Nysa 8 Plate VII

Obv.: Bust of Marcus Aurelius, r., laureate
Inscription: Αὐτ. Κ. Μ. Αὐρη. 'Αντωνεῖνος Σεβ.
Rev.: Men standing l. with staff and patera
Inscription: 'Επὶ γρ. 'Ασιατικοῦ Νυσαέων

> Bibliography: none

Weight: 8.13 gr. (Munich)
Illustrated example: Munich
Remarks: Similar to the preceding, but smaller denomination.

Nysa 9   Plate VII

Obv.:   Bust of Marcus Aurelius, r., as Augustus, laureate
Inscription: A. K. M. Αὐρ. ʼΑντωνεῖνος Σεβ.
Rev.:   Men standing l., with staff in l. hand, patera in r.
Inscription: ʼΕπὶ γρ. Αὐρ. Διοδότου Νυσαέων

> Bibliography:
> Drexler, col. 2705
> Regling, *Nysa*, p. 82, no. 89

Weight: 22.79 gr. (Berlin)
Illustrated example: Berlin
Remarks: I have retained the identification as given in the Berlin collection, but this may turn out to be a variant of Nysa 14 (Commodus).

Nysa 10   Plate VII

Obv.:   Bust of Lucius Verus, r., laureate
Inscription: Αὐρ. Οὐῆρος
Rev.:   Men standing l. with patera in r. hand, staff in l.
Inscription: ʼΕπὶ γρ. ʼΑσιατικοῦ Νυσαέων

> Bibliography:
> Regling, *Nysa*, p. 83, no. 103

Weight: 8.49 gr. (Berlin)
Illustrated example: Berlin

Nysa 11   Plate VII

Obv.:   Bust of Lucius Verus, r., laureate
Inscription: Αὐρ. Οὐῆρος
Rev.:   Men standing l., with patera in r. hand, staff in l.
Inscription: ʼΕπὶ στ. Κρατικοῦ ..... Νυσαέων

> Bibliography:
> Lane, II, p. 19, no. 7 and Pl. III, 10

Weight: 14.48 gr. (Vienna)
Illustrated example: Vienna

COINS 23

Nysa 12 Plate VIII

Obv.: Marcus Aurelius and Lucius Verus standing facing each other and shaking hands
Inscription: Αὐτοκράτορας Καισαρ. ᾿Αντωνεῖνον καὶ Οὔῆρον
Rev.: Men standing l. with patera in r. hand, staff in l.
Inscription: ᾿Επὶ γρ. Αὐρ. Διοδότου Νυσαέων (with variations in spelling)

    Bibliography:
    Drexler, col. 2705
    BMC Lydia, p. 178, no. 52
    Hunt., II, p. 459, Nysa 4
    Regling, *Nysa*, p. 82, no. 93
    Lane, II, p. 19, Nysa 8, and Pl. IV, no. 1

Weight: 21.74 gr. (Glasgow) - 26.39 gr. (Vienna)
Illustrated example: London

Nysa 13 Plate VIII

Obv.: Bust of Marcus Aurelius, r., laureate
Inscription: Αὐτ. Κ. Μ. Αὐρη. ᾿Αντωνεῖνος Σε.
Rev.: Men standing frontally with patera and staff in hexastyle temple
Inscription: ᾿Επὶ γρ. ᾿Ασιατικοῦ Νυσαέων

    Bibliography:
    Birch, *NC*, 1841, p. 141, no. 1
    Drexler, col. 2706
    BMC Lydia, p. 177, no. 39 and Pl. XX, no. 6 (rev. only)
    Inv. Wadd., *RN*, 1897, p. 439, no. 2504
    Hunt., II, p. 459, Nysa 3
    Regling, *Nysa*, p. 82, no. 84
    SNG Aulock, Pl. 97, no. 3046
    Lane, II, p. 20, no. 20

Weight: 19.89 gr. (Glasgow) - 25.01 gr. (Paris)
Illustrated example: Paris

Nysa 14 Plate VIII

Obv.: Bust of Commodus, l., laureate
Inscription: Αὐτ. Καῖσαρ Μ. Αὐρ. ᾿Αντ. Κόμμοδος Σεβ.

Rev.: Men standing l. with patera in r. hand, staff in l.
Inscription: 'Επὶ γρ. Αὐρ. Διοδότου Νυσαέων

> Bibliography:
> Hunt., II, p. 460, Nysa 5
> Regling, Nysa, p. 84, no. 112. Lane II, Nysa 9, Pl. IV, 2

Weight: 20.10 gr. (Paris) - 21.88 gr. (Glasgow)
Illustrated example: Glasgow

Nysa 15   Plate VIII

Obv.: Bust of Elagabalus, r., radiate
Inscription: 'Αντωνεῖνος Καῖσαρ
Rev.: Bust of Men, r.
Inscription: Νυσαέων

> Bibliography:
> J. G. Milne, NC, 1939, p. 192, Nysa 3 and Pl. IX, 2
> Lane, II, p. 19, Nysa 10 and Pl. IV, no. 3

Weight: 3.29 gr.
Illustrated example: Oxford
Remarks: I have given above the description of the coin first made by Milne, and supported by Professor C. M. Kraay, but I remain unhappy about it. The size and style of the coin seem out of place in the Severan period. Particularly striking is the resemblance of the rev. bust of Men to the early issues of Bageis.

Nysa 16   Plate IX

Obv.: Bust of Elagabalus, r. laureate
Inscription: Αὐ Κ. Μ. Αὐρ. 'Αντωνεῖνος
Rev.: Men standing l. with patera in r. hand, staff in l.
Inscription: Γρ. Αὐρ. Θεοτείμου Νυσαέων

> Bibliography:
> BMC Lydia, p. 180, no. 51, Pl. XX, no. 9 (rev. only)
> Regling, Nysa, p. 85, no. 125
> Weber, III, i, pp. 448-9 and Pl. 243, no. 6869
> Lane, II, p. 19, no. 11

Weight: 30.89 gr. (Paris) - 33.51 gr. (London)
Illustrated example: Weber

Nysa 17 Plate IX

Obv.: Bust of Elagabalus, r., laureate
Inscription: Αὐ. Κ. Μ. Αὐρ. ᾿Αντωνεῖνος
Rev.: Men standing l. with patera in r. hand, staff in l.
Inscription: Γρ. Αὐρ. ᾿Ιουλιανοῦ Νυσαέων

   Bibliography: none

Weight: 24.25 gr. (New York)
Illustrated example: New York

Nysa 18 Plate IX

Obv.: Bust of Elagabalus, r., laureate
Inscription: Αὐ. Κ. Μ. Αὐρη. ᾿Αντωνεῖνος
Rev.: Men standing l. with patera and staff in tetrastyle temple with arch over head
Inscription: ᾿Επ. γρ. Αὐρ. Θεοτείμου Νυσαέων

   Bibliography:
   Regling, *Nysa*, p. 85, no. 126 and Pl. XIII (rev. only)
   SNG Cop., *Lydia*, Pl. X, no. 321
   Lane, II, p. 20, Nysa no. 21

Weight: 11.49 gr. (Cop) - 13.42 gr. (Paris)
Illustrated example: Copenhagen

Nysa 19 Plate IX

Obv.: Bust of Elagabalus, r., laureate
Inscription: Αὐτ. Κ. Αὐρ. ᾿Αντωνῖνος
Rev.: Tyche standing r., with mural crown, Men-statuette on outstretched right hand, and bunch of grapes
Inscription: Νυσαέων

   Bibliography:
   Drexler, *Z. für N.*, 1887, p. 83
   Regling, *Nysa*, p. 85, no. 129
   Drexler, col. 2706
   Lane, II, p. 20, note 14

Weight: 6.22 gr. (Athens)
Illustrated example: Athens

Nysa 20 Plate IX

Obv.: Bust of Julia Maesa, r.
Inscription: 'Ιου. Μαι. Σεβα.
Rev.: Men standing l., with patera in r. hand, staff in l.
Inscription: Νυσαέων

> Bibliography:
> Regling, *Nysa*, p. 85, no. 135
> *SNG Cop.*, *Lydia*, Pl. X, no. 322

Weight: 6.44 gr. (Copenhagen) - 6.73 gr. (Athens)
Illustrated example: Athens

Nysa 21

Obv.: Bust of Julia Maesa, r.
Inscription: 'Ιου. Μαι. Σεβα.
Rev.: Tyche standing with Men-statuette and bunch of grapes
Inscription: Νυσαέων

> Bibliography:
> Drexler, *Z. für N.*, 1887, p. 83
> Drexler, col. 2706
> Regling, *Nysa*, p. 85. no. 136
> Lane, II, p. 20, note 14

Weight: unavailable
Illustrated example: none
Remarks: This coin is listed by Regling with hesitation from old and unreliable sources, and should perhaps be excluded.

Nysa 22 Plate IX

Obv.: Bust of Severus Alexander, r.
Inscription: Αὐ. Κ. 'Αλέξανδρος Καῖσαρ
Rev.: Tyche standing facing with mural crown, Men-statuette in l. hand, bunch of grapes in r.
Inscription: 'Επὶ γρ. Αὐρ. 'Αμμιανοῦ Νυσαέων

> Bibliography:
> Wroth, *NC*, 1905, p. 340, and Pl. XV, 6 (rev. only)
> Regling, *Nysa*, p. 85, no. 137 and Pl. XIII (rev. only)
> Lane, II, p. 20, no. 23

Weight: 12.50 gr. (London)
Illustrated example: London

Nysa 23
Plate X

Obv.: Bust of Maximinus, r., laureate
Inscription: Γ. 'Ιου. Ούη. Μαξιμεῖνος
Rev.: Men standing l. with patera in r. hand, staff in l.
Inscription: Νυσαέων

> Bibliography:
> Regling, *Nysa*, p. 86, no. 148
> *SNG Aulock*, Pl. 97, no. 3050
> *SNG Fitz.*, Pl. 95, no. 4870
> Lane, II, p. 19, no. 13: III, p. 104, no. 5

Weight: 5.41 gr. (Aulock) - 6.15 gr. (Cambridge)
Illustrated example: Aulock

Nysa 24
Plate X

Obv.: Bust of Maximus, r., laureate
Inscription: Γ. 'Ιουλ. Οὐῆρος Μάξιμος Και.
Rev.: Men standing l. with patera in r. hand, staff in l.
Inscription: 'Επὶ γρ. Μ. Αὐρ. Εὐτύχου β' ῎Ιφωνος Νυσαέων

> Bibliography:
> *SNG Aulock*, Pl. 97, no. 3052
> Lane, II, p. 19, no. 14

Weight: 15.24 gr. (Aulock)
Illustrated example: Aulock

Nysa 25
Plate X

Obv.: Bust of Gordian III, r., laureate
Inscription: Αὐτ. Κ. Μ. 'Αντ. Γορδιανὸς Αὐ.
Rev.: Men standing l. with patera in r. hand, staff in l. Bull's head at feet under patera.
Inscription: 'Επὶ γρ. Μ. Αὐρ. Εὐφήμου β' Νυσαέων

> Bibliography:
> Roscher, p. 143 and Pl. Ia, no. 14 (rev. only)

Drexler, col. 2705
BMC Lydia, p. 181, no. 58
Regling, Nysa, p. 87, no. 166
Lane, II, p. 19, Nysa 15

Weight: 23.42 gr. (Berlin) - 18.00 gr. (London)
Illustrated example: Berlin

Nysa 26   Plate X

Obv.: Bust of Gordian III, r., laureate
Inscription: Αὐτ. Κ. Μ. ʼΑν. Γορδιανός
Rev.: Men standing l. with pine-cone in r. hand, staff in l.
Inscription: Νυσαέων

Bibliography:
Kraft, Pl. 18, no. 70b

Weight: 4.54 gr. (Boston)
Illustrated example: Boston

Nysa 27   Plate X

Obv.: Bust of Gordian III, r., laureate
Inscription: Αὐτ. Κ. Μ. ʼΑντ. Γορδιανὸς Αὐγ. (with variations)
Rev.: Men standing l. with pine-cone in r. hand, staff in l.
Inscription: ʼΕπὶ γρ. Αὐρ. ʼΑττικοῦ δʼ Νυσαέων (with variations)

Bibliography:
Drexler, col. 2705
Regling, Nysa, p. 87, no. 161
Lane, II, p. 19, Nysa 15
Kraft, Pl. 18, 75c

Weight: 16.07 gr. (Berlin) - 17.34 gr. (Munich)
Illustrated example: Munich

Nysa 28   Plate XI

Obv.: Bust of Philip I., r., radiate
Inscription: Αὐ. Καῖσαρ ʼΙου. Φίλιππος Σε.
Rev.: Men standing l. with patera in r. hand, staff in l., bull's head at feet
Inscription: Γρ. Αὐρ. ʼΑρτεμιδώρου τοῦ Μελιτῶνος βʼ Νυσαέων

Bibliography:
Inv. Wadd., RN, 1897, p. 439, no. 2059
Regling, Nysa, p. 88, no. 173
Lane, II, p. 19, no. 16 and Pl. IV, no. 4

Weight: 17.36 gr. (Paris)
Illustrated example: Paris

Nysa 29   Plate XI

Obv.: Bust of Philip I., r., radiate
Inscription: Αὐ. Καῖσαρ ’Ιου. Φίλιππος Σε.
Rev.: Men recumbent, facing l., patera in r. hand, as a river-god
Inscription: Γρ. ’Ιουλ. Πετρ. Ζωτικοῦ Φιλ. Νυσαέων

Bibliography:
Drexler, col. 2706
Regling, Nysa, p. 88, note 1
Lane, II, p. 20, no. 25 and Pl. V, 1

Weight: 22.52 gr.
Illustrated example: Oxford

Remarks: There must have been some specific occasion for the unusual representation of this unique coin, about which both Regling and Drexler entertained doubts.

Nysa 30   Plate XI

Obv.: Busts of Philip I and Philip II, facing each other
Inscription: largely illegible
Rev.: Men (?) standing in hexastyle temple. Coin very badly worn.
Inscription: ’Επ. γρ. Τρυφωντ. Μοσχίωνος Νυσαέων

Bibliography:
Regling, Nysa, p. 88, no. 174
Lane, II, p. 20, Nysa 22, and Pl. IV, 8 (rev. only)

Weight: 16.29 gr. (Berlin)
Illustrated example: Berlin

Remarks: This coin seems to be known only from one example, and that badly worn. There are serious doubts in my mind as to whether Men is actually portrayed, which can only be resolved if a better preserved example of the coin is found.

Nysa 31 Plate XI

Obv.: Bust of Valerian, r., laureate
Inscription: Αὐτ. Κ. Πο. Λικιν. Οὐαλεριανός
Rev.: Men standing l. with patera in r. hand, staff in l., bull's head at feet
Inscription: Ἐπὶ γρ. Μενάνδρου β' Νυσαέων (with variations)

> Bibliography:
> Drexler, col. 2705
> *BMC Lydia*, Nysa no. 67
> Regling, *Nysa*, p. 89, no. 192
> Lane, II, p. 19, Nysa 17, and Pl. IV, no. 5

Weight: 16.90 gr. (London) - 23.25 gr. (Paris)
Illustrated example: London

Nysa 32 Plate XII

Obv.: Bust of Valerian, r., laureate
Inscription: Αὐτ Κ. Πο. Λικιν. Οὐαλεριανός
Rev.: Men standing l. patera in r. hand and staff in l., bull's head at feet
Inscription: Ἐπὶ γρ. Ζωτικοῦ Φιλαργ. Νυσαέων

> Bibliography:
> Drexler, col. 2705
> Regling, *Nysa*, p. 89, no. 187

Weight: 7.73 gr. (Berlin) - 9.11 gr. (London)
Illustrated example: Berlin

Nysa 33 Plate XII

Obv.: Bust of Valerian, r., laureate
Inscription: Αὐτ. Κ. Πο. Λικιν. Βαλεριανός
Rev.: Men standing l. with patera in r. hand and staff in l., bull's head at feet
Inscription: Τρυφωσιανοῦ Ἀριστάνδρου Νυσαέων

> Bibliography:
> Imhoof, *Gr. M.*, p. 719, no. 602
> Drexler, col. 2705-6
> Regling, *Nysa*, p. 89, no. 201

Weight: 7.88 gr. (Vienna)
Illustrated example: Vienna

Nysa 34 Plate XII

Obv.: Bust of Valerian, r., laureate
Inscription: Αὐτ. Κ. Π. Λικιν. Βαλεριανός
Rev.: Men standing l. with patera and staff
Inscription: Ἐπὶ γρ. Μ. Αὐρ. Λαιανοῦ Νυσαέων

   Bibliography: none

Weight: 8.74 gr. (Munich) - 9.23 gr. (Vienna)
Illustrated example: Vienna

Nysa 35 Plate XII

Obv.: Bust of Valerian, r., laureate
Inscription: Αὐτ. Κ. Πο. Λικιν. Βαλεριανός
Rev.: Tyche standing l. with kalathos, Men-statuette on r. hand, and cornucopia
Inscription: Ἐπὶ γρ. Αἰλ. Πρόκλου Νυσαέων

   Bibliography:
   Roscher, Pl. Ib, no. 16 (rev. only)
   Drexler, col. 2706
   BMC Lydia, p. 184, nos. 69 and 70
   Regling, *Nysa*, p. 89, no. 194 and Pl. XIII (rev. only)
   Lane, II, p. 20, no. 24

Weight: 8.12 gr.-8.73 gr. (London)
Illustrated example: Berlin

Nysa 36 Plate XII

Obv.: Bust of Valerian r., laureate
Inscription: Αὐτ. Κ. Σο. Λικιν. Βαλεριανός
Rev.: Tyche standing with Men-statuette and cornucopia
Inscription: Ἐπ. γρ. Αὐρ. Τρυφωσιανοῦ Ἀρ. Νυσαέων

   Bibliography:
   Inv. Wadd., RN, 1897, p. 439, no. 2514
   Regling, *Nysa*, p. 90, no. 203

Weight: 8.83 gr. (Paris)
Illustrated example: Paris

Nysa 37 — Plate XII

Obv.: Bust of Gallienus, r., laureate
Inscription: Πο. Λικιν. Γαλλιηνὸς Κ.
Rev.: Men standing l. with patera in r. hand, staff in l.
Inscription: Νυσαέων

> Bibliography:
> Regling, *Nysa*, p. 90, no. 216
> Lane, II, p. 20, no. 18 and Pl. IV, no. 6 (rev. only)

Weight: 4.53 gr. (Berlin)
Illustrated example: Berlin

Nysa 38 — Plate XII

Obv.: Bust of Gallienus, r., laureate
Inscription: Αὐτ. Κ. Πο. Λι. Γαλλιηνός
Rev.: Men standing l. with patera in r. hand, staff in l., bull's head at feet
Inscription: Νυσαέων

> Bibliography:
> Regling, *Nysa*, p. 90, 216 (treated together with preceding)

Weight: 4.18 gr. (Berlin)
Illustrated example: Berlin

Nysa 39 — Plate XII

Obv.: Bust of Gallienus, r., radiate
Inscription: Πο. Λικκιννι. Γαλλιηνὸς Κ.
Rev.: Men standing l. with patera in r. hand, staff in l.
Inscription: Ἐπὶ γρ. Μενάνδρου β' Νυσαέων

> Bibliography:
> Regling, *Nysa*, p. 90, no. 207
> Lane, II, p. 20, no. 19 and Pl. IV, no. 7

Weight: 11.19 gr. (Gotha)
Illustrated example: Gotha

Nysa 40 Plate XII

Obv.: Bust of Gallienus, r., laureate
Inscription: Αὐτ. Κ. Πο. Λικινν. Γαλλιηνός
Rev.: Tyche standing l. with kalathos, Men-statuette, and cornucopia
Inscription: 'Επὶ γρ. Κλ. Πολλίωνος Νυσαέων

> Bibliography:
> Drexler, col. 2706
> Regling, *Nysa*, p. 90, no. 211
> *SNG Cop., Lydia*, Pl. X, no. 335

Weight: 8.05 gr. (Copenhagen)
Illustrated example: Copenhagen

Nysa 41 Plate XIII

Alliance coin of Nysa and Ephesus
Obv.: Bust of Elagabalus, r., laureate
Inscription: Αὐ. Κ. Μ. Αὐρ. 'Αντωνεῖνος
Rev.: Men on r., standing l. with patera and staff. Ephesian Artemis on l. between two stags.
Inscription: 'Επὶ γρ. Αὐρ. 'Αριστάνδρου Νυσαέων καὶ 'Εφεσίων ὁμόνοια

> Bibliography:
> Regling, *Nysa*, p. 85, no. 124 and Pl. XIII (rev. only)
> Lane, II, p. 20, no. 26

Weight: 25.67 gr. (Munich)
Illustrated example: Munich

Nysa 42 Plate XIII

Alliance coin of Nysa and Sparta
Obv.: Bust of Maximinus, r., laureate
Inscription: ... Οὐηρ .... Μαξ .... (largely effaced)
Rev.: Men on r., standing l. with patera and staff, bull's head at feet. At l., standing r., archaic statue of Ares.
Inscription: 'Επὶ γ. 'Αρτεμιδώρου τοῦ Μελιτῶνος ὁμόνοια Νυσαέων καὶ Λακεδαιμονίων

Bibliography:
Inv. Wadd., RN, 1898, p. 601, no. 7052 (attributed to Tabai)
Lane, II, p. 20, no. 27 and Pl. IV, no. 2

Weight: 49.22 gr. (Paris)
Illustrated example: Paris

Nysa 43   Plate XIII

Alliance coin of Nysa and Sparta
Obv.: Bust of Marcus Aurelius, r., laureate
Inscription: .... Ἀντωνεῖνος
Rev.: Men standing at l., Zeus standing at r.
Inscription: [Λακεδαιμο]νίων καὶ Ν[υσαέων ἐπὶ ἄρχοντος τοῦ δεῖνα] ὁμόνοια

Bibliography: none

Weight: 17.79 gr. (broken)
Remarks: I know this coin only from a broken copy in the collection of the Institut für Numismatik und vorislamische Geschichte Mittelasiens Vienna. The attribution is made with due reservation on the basis of the preceding coin.

Saitta 1   Plate XIII

Obv.: Bust of Zeus Patrios, r.
Inscription: Ζεὺς Πάτριος
Rev.: Men standing l. with pine-cone and staff, feet far apart, r. hand far outstretched
Inscription: Ἐπὶ Κλ. Μαχαιρίωνος Σαιττηνῶν

Bibliography:
Imhoof, Gr. M., p. 721, no. 613
Drexler, col. 2707
BMC Lydia, Saitta 4
SNG Aulock, Pl. 98, no. 3087
Lane, II, p. 21, Saitta 1

Weight: 7.35 gr. (Aulock) - 8.97 gr. (London)
Illustrated example: Aulock

COINS 35

Saitta 2 Plate XIII

Obv.: Bust of Zeus Patrios, r.
Inscription: Ζεὺς Πάτριος
Rev.: Men standing l. with pine-cone and staff, feet far apart, r. hand far outstretched
Inscription: 'Επὶ 'Οκτα. Κίνβρου ἀρχ. Σαιττηνῶν

> Bibliography:
> S. Birch *NC*, 1841, p. 138, no. 2
> *BMC Lydia*, p. 213, Saitta 5
> *SNG Aulock*, Pl. 115, no. 3251 (attributed to Brouzos)

Weight: 8.27 gr. (London) - 10.41 gr. (Aulock)
Illustrated example: Athens
Note: For the reading Κίνβρου cf. Imhoof, *Kl. M.*, II, p. 523.

Saitta 3 Plate XIV

Obv.: Bust of Roma, r.
Inscription: Σαιττηνῶν
Rev.: Men standing l. with patera and staff
Inscription: 'Επὶ 'Οκτα. Κίνβρου ἀρχ. Σαιττηνῶν

> Bibliography: none

Weight: 9.48 gr. (Berlin)
Illustrated example: Berlin

Saitta 4 Plate XIV

Obv.: Bust of Men, r., with starry cap
Inscription: 'Αξιοττηνός (variation in division)
Rev.: River god Hermus, recumbent, head to r.
Inscription: Σαιττηνῶν ῞Ερμος

> Bibliography:
> Roscher, Pl. Ia, no. 5 (obv. only)
> Drexler, col. 2707
> Imhoof-Blumer, *SNR*, VI, 1896, p. 278, no. 1
> *BMC Lydia*, p. 216, no. 23 and Pl. XXIII, no. 5
> *SNG Aulock*, Pl. 98, no. 3089
> Lane, II, p. 21, no. 9

Weight: 4.10 gr. (London) - 5.57 gr. (Aulock)
Illustrated example: Aulock
Remarks: Axiottenos also appears as a by-name for Men in the inscriptions from the area of near-by Kula, and would appear to be from Axitta, a place-name probably referring to the whole area.

Saitta 5   Plate XIV

Obv.: Bust of Men, r., with starry cap
Inscription: Ἀξιοττηνός
Rev.: River god Hyllos, recumbent, head to r.
Inscription: Σαιττηνῶν Ὕλλος

> Bibliography:
> Imhoof-Blumer, *SNR*, 1896, p. 278, no. 2
> *BMC Lydia*, p. 216, no. 24
> Imhoof-Blumer, *SNR*, 1913, p. 55, no. 169 and Pl. II, no. 17
> *SNG Cop.-, Lydia*, Pl. XII, no. 396

Weight: 3.33 gr. (Copenhagen) - 5.52 gr. (Imhoof)
Illustrated example: Copenhagen

Saitta 6   Plate XIV

Obv.: Bust of Men, r., starry cap
Inscription: Ἀξιοττηνός
Rev.: Dionysus standing l. with kantharos and thyrsos, panther at feet
Inscription: Σαιττηνῶν

> Bibliography:
> Drexler, col. 2707
> *BMC Lydia*, p. 214, nos. 15-16
> Lane, II, p. 21, no. 11 and Pl. V, no. 4

Weight: 3.39 gr. (London) - 5.58 gr. (Budapest)
Illustrated example: Budapest

COINS 37

Saitta 7 Plate XIV

Obv.: Bust of Men, r. Apparently no stars on cap.
No inscription
Rev.: Apollo, nude except for chlamys over shoulder, with bow, legs crossed
Inscription: Σαιττηνῶν

> Bibliography:
> *BMC Lydia*, p. 215, no. 17
> Grose, III, p. 222, no. 8701 and Pl. 305, no. 10
> Lane, II, p. 21, no. 12

Weight: 3.05 (London) - 3.48 gr. (Cambridge)
Illustrated example: Cambridge

Saitta 8 Plate XIV

Obv.: Bust of Marcus Aurelius, r., as Caesar, bareheaded
Inscription: Μ. Αὐρήλιος Οὐῆρος Καῖσαρ
Rev.: Men standing l. with pine-cone and staff
Inscription: 'Επὶ Φλ. 'Ηρκλανου Σαιττηνῶν

> Bibliography:
> *SNG Aulock*, Pl. 99, no. 3094

Weight: 25.95 gr. (Aulock)
Illustrated example: Aulock

Saitta 9 Plate XIV

Obv.: Bust of Septimius Severus, r., laureate
Inscription: Αὐ. Κ. Λ. Σεπ. Σεουῆρος Περ.
Rev.: Men standing l. with pine-cone and staff
Inscription: 'Επὶ 'Ανδρονείκου ἀρχ. α' Σαιττηνῶν (with various arrangements)

> Bibliography:
> Drexler, col. 2707
> *Inv. Wadd., RN*, 1898, p. 364, no. 5176
> *BMC Lydia*, pp. 219-220, nos. 42-43 and Pl. XXIII, 8
> Hübl, II, p. 311, no. 3528
> *SNG Aulock*, Pl. 99, no. 3098

Lane, II, p. 21, no. 3
Kraft, Pl. 69, no. 50a

Weight: 6.74 gr. (London) - 10.26 gr. (Berlin)
Illustrated example: Aulock

Saitta 10   Plate XV

Obv.:   Bust of Septimius Severus, r., laureate
Inscription: Αὐτ. Κ. Λ. Σεπ. Σεουῆρος Περ.
Rev.:   Men on l., standing r. with pine-cone and staff, facing a seated Cybele. There are lions at the bottom of Cybele's throne.
Inscription: Ἐπὶ Ἀνδρονείκου Διοδωρ... Σαιττηνῶν

> Bibliography:
> Imhoof-Blumer, *SNR*, 1913, p. 56, no. 161
> Lane, II, p. 21, no. 13 and Pl. IV, no. 5
> H. Bloesch, *Antike Kleinkunst in Winterthur*, p. 63, no. 434 and Pl. XXIII

Weight: 40.50 gr. (Berlin) - 51.64 gr. (Winterthur)
Illustrated example: Winterthur
Remarks: The reverses of this and the following similar coins of the reigns of Caracalla and Elagabalus remind one of the inscriptions of the nearby area of Kula, in which Men is honored together with a female divinity.

Saitta 11   Plate XV

Obv.:   Bust of Julia Domna, r.
Inscription: Ἰουλία Σεβαστή
Rev.:   Men standing l. with pine-cone and staff
Inscription: Ἐπὶ Ἀνδρονείκου ἀρχ. α' Σαιττηνῶν

> Bibliography:
> *Inv. Wadd.*, *RN*, 1898, p. 364, no. 5179
> Prowe, *NS*, II, 1913, p. 169, no. 23 and Pl. III (attributed to Adramyttium)
> Imhoof-Blumer, *SNR*, 1913, p. 56, bottom
> Grose, II, p. 223, no. 8705 and Pl. 305, no. 14
> Lane, II, p. 21, Saitta 4

Weight: 20.21 gr. (Paris) - 27.95 gr. (London)
Illustrated example: Cambridge

Saitta 12 Plate XV

Obv.: Bust of Caracalla, r., laureate
Inscription: Αὐτ. Κ. Μ. Αὐρη. ᾿Αντωνεῖνος
Rev.: Men standing l. with pine-cone and staff, between the recumbent river gods Hyllus and Hermus
Inscription: ᾿Επὶ ᾿Ατταλιανοῦ ἀρχ. α' Σαιττηνῶν

> Bibliography:
> Waddington, *RN*, 1852, p. 31, no. 1
> A. Engel, *RN*, 1884, p. 24, no. 9
> Drexler, col. 2707
> *BMC Lydia*, p. 220, no. 46 and Pl. XXIII, no. 9 (rev. only)
> *Inv. Wadd.*, *RN*, 1898, p. 364, no. 5182
> *SNG Aulock*, Pl. 284, no. 8249
> Lane, II, p. 21, no. 7

Weight: 19.24 gr. (Paris) - 23.50 gr. (London)
Illustrated example: Istanbul

Saitta 13 Plate XV

Obv.: Bust of Caracalla(?), r., youthful, laureate
Inscription: .... Και. Μ. ... Αὐ. ᾿Αν. ....
Rev.: Men with pine-cone, standing before throned Cybele. His l. hand is raised (in greeting?)
Inscription obscure

> Bibliography: none

Weight: 51.65 gr. (Hecht)
Illustrated example: Hecht collection

Saitta 14 Plate XVI

Obv.: Bust of Elagabalus, r., laureate
Inscription: Αὐτ. Κ. Μ. Αὐρ. ᾿Αντωνεῖνος
Rev.: Men on l. standing r. before Cybele, who sits on throne at r., holding a patera
Inscription: ᾿Επὶ Φαβ. Γαίου ἀρχ. α' τό β' Σαιττηνῶν

> Bibliography:
> Imhoof-Blumer, *SNR*, 1908, p. 17, no. 2 and Pl. VI, no. 4
> Lane, II, p. 22, no. 14 and Pl. V, no. 6

Weight: 20.94 gr. (Berlin)
Illustrated example: Berlin

Saitta 15   Plate XVI

Obv.: Bust of Severus Alexander, r., laureate
Inscription: Αὐτ. Κ. Μ. Αὐρ. Σεβ. Ἀλέξανδρος
Rev.: Men standing l. with pine-cone and staff
Inscription: Ἐπὶ Μ. Κλ. Φ. Βηδ. Ῥουφείνου ἀρχ. α' Σαιττηνῶν

> Bibliography:
> Drexler, col. 2707
> *SNG Aulock*, Pl. 99, no. 3102
> Lane, II, p. 21, no. 5

Weight: 19.03 gr. (Aulock)
Illustrated example: Aulock

Saitta 16   Plate XVI

Obv.: Bust of Maximinus, r., laureate
Inscription: Αὐτ. Κ. Γ. Ἰου. Μαξιμεῖνος Σεβ.
Rev.: Men standing l. with pine-cone and staff
Inscription: Ἐπὶ Μ. Ἀντ. Ἀλεξάνδρου ἀρχ. α' Σαιττηνῶν

> Bibliography:
> *BMC Lydia*, p. 223, no. 57
> Lane, II, p. 21, no. 6 and Pl. V, no. 3
> Artemis Antiquities, cat. VI, no. 431

Weight: 20.59 gr. (London)
Illustrated example: London

Saitta 17   Plate XVI

Obv.: Bust of Gordian III, r., laureate
Inscription: Αὐτ. Κ. Μ. Ἀντ. Γορδιανός
Rev.: Men standing l. with pine-cone and staff between Hyllus and Hermus
Inscription: Ἐπὶ Αὐρ. Αἰ. Ἀτταλιανοῦ υἱοῦ ἰπάσου Σαιττηνῶν ἀρχ. α' τὸ β'

Bibliography:
Torino, Monete Greche, p. 311, no. 4386
Drexler, col. 2707
BMC Lydia, p. 223, no. 58 and Pl. XXIII, no. 12 (rev. only)
Lane, II, p. 21, no. 8

Weight: 18.75 gr. (London) - 24.89 gr. (Paris)
Illustrated example: Paris
Remarks: Apparently the same man when archon for the second time (or his son?) repeats his earlier type.

Saitta 18   Plate XVII

Obv.: Bust of Philip I, r., laureate
Inscription: Αὐτ. Κ. Μ. 'Ιουλ. Φίλιππος Αὐγ.
Rev.: Men standing l. with pine-cone and staff between Hyllus and Hermus
Inscription: 'Επὶ Αὐρ. Σεπ. 'Αρ. 'Α. 'Υ 'Ασικρ. Σαιττηνῶν

Bibliography: none

Weight: 19.77 gr. (London)
Illustrated example: London

Sardis 1   Plate XVII

Obv.: Bust of Men, r.
Inscription: Μὴν 'Ασκαηνός
Rev.: Rudder and cornucopia crossed
Inscription: Σαρδιανῶν β' Νεωκόρων

Bibliography:
Roscher, Pl. Ia, no. 3 (obv. only)
Drexler, col. 2707
BMC Lydia, p. 250, no. 95 and Pl. XXVI, no. 3
Lane, II, p. 22, Sardis 1

Weight: 4.58 gr. (London) - 6.37 gr. (Athens)
Illustrated example: Athens

Sardis 2   Plate XVII

Obv.: Bust of Men, r.
Inscription: Μὴν 'Ασκαηνός

Rev.: Torch and cornucopia crossed
Inscription: Σαρδιανῶν β' Νεωκόρων

> Bibliography:
> Drexler, col. 2707
> *Inv. Wadd., RN*, 1898, p. 367, no. 5218

Weight: 3.93 gr.- 6.42 gr. (Paris)
Illustrated example: Paris

Sardis 3   Plate XVII

Obv.: Bust of Men, r.
Inscription: Μὴν Ἀσκαηνός
Rev.: Reclining river-god Hermus, head r.
Inscription: Σαρδιανῶν β' Νεωκόρων Ἕρμος

> Bibliography:
> Drexler, col. 2707
> *SNG Cop., Lydia*, Pl. 15, no. 511
> Lane, II, p. 22, Sardis 2

Weight: 4.76 gr. (Paris) - 5.72 gr. (Athens)
Illustrated example: Athens
Remarks: Mionnet, Suppl. 7, 412, 426 ostensibly has a copy of this without β'.

Sardis 4   Plate XVII

Obv.: Bust of Men, r.
Inscription: Μὴν Ἀσκαηνός
Rev.: Sheaf of wheat
Inscription: Σαρδιανῶν β' Νεωκόρων

> Bibliography:
> Drexler, col. 2707
> *BMC Lydia*, p. 250, no. 96
> *Inv. Wadd., RN*, 1898, p. 367, no. 5217
> *SNG Cop., Lydia*, Pl. XV, no. 512
> Lane, II, p. 22, Sardis 3

Weight: 4.01 gr. (Paris) - 4.40 gr. (London)
Illustrated example: Copenhagen
Remarks: Mionnet, Suppl. 7, 412, 427, ostensibly has a copy with Σαρδιανῶν γ' Νεωκόρων.

Sardis 5 Plate XVII

Obv.: Bust of Men, r.
Inscription: 'Επὶ Τ. Κλαυ. Φιλείνου Στρ.
Rev.: Wreath surrounding inscription in three lines: Σαρδιανῶν

> Bibliography:
> Drexler, col. 2707
> Imhoof-Blumer, *SNR*, 1896, p. 289, no. 9

Weight: 3.14 gr. (Gotha)
Illustrated example: Gotha
Remarks: Imhoof-Blumer, *SNR*, 1908, p. 18, Sardis 3 presents an interesting version of this coin, with its obverse inscription counterclockwise, overstruck on a coin of Sardis from the reign of Nero. (3.02 gr.)

Sardis 6 Plate XVII

Obv.: Bust of Senate, r.
Inscription: Ἱερὰ Σύγκλητος
Rev.: Men standing l. with pine-cone and staff
Inscription: Σαρδιανῶν β' Νεωκόρων

> Bibliography:
> *BMC Lydia*, p. 248, no. 84

Weight: 4.25 gr. (Berlin)
Illustrated example: Berlin

Sardis 7 Plate XVII

Obv.: Bust of Vespasian, r.
Inscription: Αὐτοκ. Καισ. Οὐεσπασιανῷ
Rev.: Men standing l., holding pine-cone and staff, before a blazing altar
Inscription: 'Επὶ Φλ. Εἰσιγόνου Σαρδιανῶν

> Bibliography:
> Fiorelli, *Medagliere di Napoli*, no. 8570
> Drexler, col. 2707
> *Inv. Wadd.*, *RN*, 1898, p. 368, no. 5248
> J. G. Milne, *NC*, 1939, Sardis 14 and Pl. IX, 4
> Lane, II, p. 22, no. 4 and Pl. VI, no. 1

Weight: 6.85 gr. (Oxford) - 7.10 gr. (Naples)
Illustrated example: Paris

Sardis 8   Plate XVII

Obv.:   Bust of Julia Domna, r.
Inscription: Ἰουλία Σεβαστή
Rev.:   Men standing l. with pine-cone and staff
Inscription: Ἐπὶ Ῥούφου Σαρδιανῶν β′ Νεωκόρων

> Bibliography:
> Roscher, Pl. Ia, no. 17 (rev. only)
> Drexler, col. 2707
> *SNG Fitz.*, Pl. 96, no. 4886

Weight: 4.32 gr. (Gotha) - 6.44 gr. (Paris)
Illustrated example: Cambridge
Remarks: The crescent is unclear on all examples except that in Vienna.

Sardis 9   Plate XVIII

Obv.:   Bust of Julia Domna, r.
Inscription: Ἰουλία Σεβαστή
Rev.:   Men standing l. with pine-cone and staff, altar at feet
Inscription: Σαρδιανῶν β′ Νεωκόρων

> Bibliography: none

Weight: 5.50 gr. (Vienna) - 6.46 gr. (Paris)
Illustrated example: Vienna

Sardis 10   Plate XVIII

Obv.:   Bust of Julia Mamaea, r.
Inscription: Ἰου. Μαμαῖα
Rev.:   Men standing l. with pine-cone and staff
Inscription: Σαρδιανῶν β′ Νεωκόρων

> Bibliography:
> Drexler, col. 2707
> *Inv. Wadd.*, *RN*, 1898, p. 370, no. 5270
> Lane, II, p. 22, no. 6 and Pl. VI, no. 2

Weight: 5.19 gr.-5.70 gr. (Paris)
Illustrated example: Paris
Remarks: Crescent indistinct on this coin.

Sardis 11   Plate XVIII

Obv.: Bust of Julia Maesa, r.
Inscription: 'Ιουλία Μαῖσα Σε.
Rev.: Men standing l. with pine-cone and staff. The crescent is clear.
Inscription: Σαρδιανῶν τρὶς (or γ') Νεωκόρων

> Bibliography:
> BMC Lydia, Sardis, no. 174
> Kraft, Pl. 30, no. 20

Weight: 4.82 gr. (Paris) - 6.27 gr. (Istanbul)
Illustrated example: Istanbul

Sardis 12   Plate XVIII

Obv.: Bust of Tranquillina, r.
Inscription: Φουρ. Τρανκυλλεῖνα Σεβ.
Rev.: Men standing l. with pine-cone and staff. The crescent is distinct on this coin.
Inscription: Σαρδιανῶν β' Νεωκόρων

> Bibliography:
> Drexler, col. 2707
> BMC Lydia, Sardis, nos. 194-5
> Lane, II, p. 22, no. 7 and Pl. VI, no. 3

Weight: 4.66 gr. (London) - 5.83 gr. (Vienna)
Illustrated example: Vienna

Sardis 13   Plate XVIII

Alliance coin of Sardis and Hierapolis
Obv.: Female bust, r.
Inscription: 'Ιεραπολειτῶν καὶ Σαρδιανῶν
Rev.: Men standing l. with patera and staff
Inscription: Νεωκόρων 'Ομόνοια

Bibliography:
Drexler, col. 2713
E. Weber, *JIAN*, 1912, p. 88, no. III and Pl. XI, no. 11
Lane, II, p. 22, no. 8 and Pl. VI, no. 4

Weight: 3.78 gr. (Paris) - 3.99 gr. (Athens)
Illustrated example: Athens

Silandus 1   Plate XVIII

Obv.: Bust of Domitia, r.
Inscription: Δομιτία Αὐγοῦστα, counterclockwise
Rev.: Men standing l. with pine-cone and staff
Inscription: Σιλανδέων

Bibliography:
Drexler, col. 2708
BMC Lydia, Silandus 17
SNG Aulock, Pl. 285, no. 8264
Lane, II, p. 23, no. 1 and Pl. VI, no. 5

Weight: 1.77 gr. (Paris) - 3.17 gr. (Aulock)
Illustrated example: Athens

Silandus 2   Plate XVIII

Obv.: Bust of Septimius Severus, r., laureate
Inscription: Αὐ. Κα. Σ. Σεουῆρος Περ.
Rev.: Men standing l. with pine-cone and staff
Inscription: Σιλανδέων

Bibliography:
Inv. Wadd., *RN*, 1898, p. 372, no. 5290
Lane, II, p. 23, Silandus 2 and Pl. VI, no. 6

Weight: 4.31 gr. (Paris)
Illustrated example: Paris
Remarks: The example published by Imhoof-Blumer, *SNR*, 1898, p. 3, no. 10, without illustration, and having Men facing r., is actually a coin of Sillyon.

Silandus 3   Plate XVIII

Obv.: Bust of Lucius Verus, r., laureate
Inscription: Αὐ. Κ. Λ. Αὐρ. Οὐῆρος

Rev.: Demeter on l. facing r., holding poppy, ear of grain, and scepter; Men on r., facing her, with pine-cone and staff
Inscription: Ἐπ. στα. Ἀτταλιανοῦ Σιλανδέων

> Bibliography:
> Imhoof-Blumer, *SNR*, 1908, p. 20, Silandus 2

Weight: 22.01 gr. (Berlin)
Illustrated example: Berlin

Silandus 4   Plate XIX

Obv.: Bust of Maximinus, r.
Inscription: Αὐ. Μαξιμεῖνος
Rev.: Bust of Men, r.
Inscription: Σιλανδέων

> Bibliography:
> Panofka, *Abh. Berlin Akad, Phil.-Hist. Klasse*, 1854, p. 565 Pl. 2, no. 8 (rev. only)

Weight: unavailable
Illustrated example: unknown location
Remarks: I reproduce Panofka's illustration, but since the coin is not to be found in the Berlin collection, considerable doubt remains in my mind as to its genuinity.

Aphrodisias 1   Plate XIX

Obv.: Bust of the senate as a youth, r. On some dies there is a head band.
Inscription: Ἱερὰ Σύγκλητος (with varying arrangements)
Rev.: Men standing l. with patera and staff, foot on bucranium
Inscription: Ἀφροδισιέων

> Bibliography:
> *BMC Caria*, p. 34, no. 52-53 and Pl. VI, 5
> Weber, III, i, p. 348, nos. 6391-2 and Pl. 226
> *SNG Cop., Caria*, Pl. 3, no. 100
> Lane, II, p. 23, Aphrodisias 1

Weight: 7.50 gr. (Copenhagen) - 10.28 gr. (London)
Illustrated example: Copenhagen

Attouda 1 Plate XIX

Obv.: Bust of Men, r., with starry cap
Inscription: Μὴν Κάρου
Rev.: Altar, with objects on it resembling three pine-cones and two smaller altars
Inscription: 'Αττουδέων

> Bibliography:
> Roscher, Pl. Ia, no. 4
> Drexler, col. 2710
> *Inv. Wadd.*, *RN*, 1898, no. 2524
> *BMC Caria*, p. 65, nos. 18-19 and Pl. X, no. 15
> *SNG Cop.*, *Caria*, Pl. 5, no. 162
> *SNG Aulock*, Pl. 78, no. 2499
> A. Laumonier, *Les Cultes Indigènes en Carie*, Paris, 1958, Pl. no. 15
> Lane, II, p. 23, Attouda 1

Weight: 4.29 gr. (London) - 6.52 gr. (Istanbul)
Illustrated example: Istanbul

Attouda 2 Plate XIX

Obv.: Bust of Demos, r.
Inscription: Δῆμος 'Αττουδέων
Rev.: Bust of Men, r., with starry cap
Inscription: Διὰ Κλαυδιανοῦ

> Bibliography: none

Weight: 4.04 gr. (Berlin) - 5.49 gr. (Athens)
Illustrated example: Athens

Attouda 3 Plate XIX

Obv.: Bust of Boule, r.
Inscription: Βουλή
Rev.: Men standing l. with patera (?) and staff
Inscription: 'Αττουδέων

> Bibliography: none

Weight: 7.00 gr. (Berlin)
Illustrated example: Berlin

Cidrama 1 Plate XIX

Obv.: Bust of Julia Maesa, r.
Inscription: Ἰουλία Μαῖσα Σεβ.
Rev.: Men standing l. with patera and staff, foot on bucranium
Inscription: Κιδραμηνῶν

> Bibliography:
> *BMC Caria*, Pl. 83, no. 10 and Pl. XIII, no. 6
> *Inv. Wadd.*, *RN*, 1898, p. 348, no. 4941 and Pl. IX, no. 7
> *SNG Aulock*, Pl. 82, no. 2591
> L. and J. Robert, *La Carie*, II, Paris, 1954, p. 345 and Pl. 62, no. 9
> L. Robert, *Villes d'Asie Mineure*, 2nd ed., Paris, 1962, p. 231, no. 13 and Pl. XI, 8
> Lane, II, p. 23, Cidrama 1

Weight: 3.35 gr. (London) - 6.00 gr. (Aulock)
Illustrated example: Athens

Trapezopolis 1 Plate XIX

Obv.: Bust of Demos, r., laureate
Inscription: Δῆμος
Rev.: Men standing l. with patera and staff; the patera is held over a lighted altar
Inscription: Τραπεζοπολειτῶν

> Bibliography:
> Drexler, col. 2698
> *BMC Caria*, p. 177, no. 2 and Pl. XXVII, 4
> *SNG Cop.*, *Caria*, Pl. XIV, 583
> Lane, II, p. 24, Trapezopolis 1
> Kraft, Pl. 114, no. 6b

Weight: 5.00 gr. (Copenhagen) - 6.45 gr. (Leningrad)
Illustrated example: Leningrad

Trapezopolis 2 Plate XIX

Obv.: Bust of Men, r.
Inscription: Τραπεζοπολειτῶν
Rev.: Winged Nemesis standing l., holding bridle
Inscription: Διὰ Πο. Αἰ. Ἀδράστου

Bibliography:
Drexler, col. 2698
BMC Caria, p. 178, no. 5 and Pl. XXVII, no. 6
Lane, II, p. 24, Trapezopolis 2

Weight: 3.70 gr. (London)
Illustrated example: London

Trapezopolis 3   Plate XIX

Obv.: Bust of Apollo, r., with quiver and lyre
Inscription: Κλαύδιος 'Ορόντης
Rev.: Bust of Men, r.
Inscription: Τραπεζοπολειτῶν

Bibliography:
Drexler, col. 2698
SNG Fitz, Pl. 92, no. 4739
Lane, II, p. 24, Trapezopolis 3 and Pl. VI, no. 7: III, p. 104, no. 3

Weight: 2.72 gr. (Cambridge) - 4.41 gr. (Paris)
Illustrated example: Cambridge

Trapezopolis 4   Plate XIX

Obv.: Bust of Men, r.
Inscription: Τραπεζοπολειτῶν
Rev.: Tyche standing l. with rudder and cornucopia
Inscription: ..... διανου

Bibliography:
BMC Caria, Trapezopolis 7

Weight: 3.19 gr. (London)
Illustrated example: London

Trapezopolis 5   Plate XX

Obv.: Bust of Septimius Severus, r., laureate
Inscription: Αὐ. Και. Λ. Σεουῆρος Περ.
Rev.: Men standing l. with patera and staff, patera over lighted altar
Inscription: Τραπεζοπολειτῶν

Bibliography:
BMC Caria, p. 179, no. 12
Lane, II, p. 24, no. 4 and Pl. VI, no. 8

Weight: 2.86 gr. (London)
Illustrated example: London

Accilaeum 1   Plate XX

Obv.: Bust of Gordian III, r., laureate
Inscription: Αὐ. Κ. Μ. 'Αντω. Γορδιανός
Rev.: Men standing r. with pine-cone and staff, foot on bucranium
Inscription: 'Ακκιλαέων

Bibliography:
H. P. Borrell, *NC*, 1845, p. 14 no. 2
Roscher, Pl. Ia, no. 15 (rev. only)
Drexler, col. 2709-10
BMC Phrygia, Accilaeum 1
Inv. Wadd., RN, 1898, p. 383, no. 5465
Svoronos, *JIAN* 1904, p. 383, no. 237 and Pl. XVII, 7 (rev. only)
SNG Cop., Phrygia, Pl. I, no. 7
SNG Aulock, Pl. 109, no. 3363
Lane, II, p. 24, Accilaeum 1
Kraft, Pl. 51, no. 7

Weight: 8.96 gr.-11.03 gr. (Paris)
Illustrated example: Aulock

Alia 1   Plate XX

Obv.: Bust of Men, r., wreath on cap
Inscription: Φροῦγι αἰτησαμένου
Rev.: Demos standing l.
Inscription: Δῆμος 'Αλιηνῶν

Bibliography:
Drexler, col. 2709
Imhoof, *Kl. M.*, I, p. 195, no. 3 and Pl. VI, no. 22
SNG Aulock, Pl. 110, no. 3386
Lane, II, p. 24, Alia 1

Weight: 3.58 gr. (Aulock) - 4.20 gr. (New York)
Illustrated example: Aulock

Alia 2   Plate XX

Obv.: Bust of Senate, r.
Inscription: Ἱερὰ Σύγκλητος
Rev.: Men standing l. with pine-cone and staff
Inscription: Αἰτησαμένου Φροῦγι 'Αλλιηνῶν

> Bibliography:
> Birch, *NC*, 1840-41, p. 98
> Drexler, col. 2709
> *BMC Phrygia*, p. 44, no. 1 and Pl. VI, 5
> Imhoof, *Kl. M.*, I, p. 195, no. 2 and Pl. VI, 21 (rev. only)
> Lane, II, p. 24, Alia 2

Weight: 6.97 gr. (London)
Illustrated example: London

Alia 3   Plate XX

Obv.: Bust of the Senate, l.
Inscription: Σύγκλητος Ἱερὰ 'Αλιην.
Rev.: Men standing l. with patera and staff
Inscription: 'Αγρεὺς ἀρχιερατε. ἀνέθηκεν.

> Bibliography:
> *Inv. Wadd.*, *RN*, 1898, p. 390, no. 5592
> Lane, II, p. 24, Alia 3 and Pl. VI, no. 9

Weight: 5.76 gr. (Paris)
Illustrated example: Paris

Alia 4   Plate XX

Obv.: Bust of Trajan, r., laureate
Inscription: Αὐτο. Νέρουα Τραιανὸς Γερμανικός
Rev.: Men on horseback, r. There is no axe, such as appears on the three following coins.
Inscription: Αἰτησαμένου Γα. 'Ασιν. Φροῦγι 'Αλιηνῶν

> Bibliography:
> *BMC Phrygia*, p. 45, no. 6
> *Inv. Wadd.*, *RN*, 1898, no. 5594
> Lane, II, p. 24, Alia 4 and Pl. VI, no. 10

Weight: 14.65 gr. (London) - 14.66 gr. (Paris)
Illustrated example: London

Alia 5 Plate XX

Obv.: Bust of Antoninus Pius, r., laureate
Inscription: Αὐτ. Καὶ. ’Αδρι. ’Αντωνεῖνος
Rev.: Men riding r. with axe over shoulder
Inscription: Γ. ’Ασιν. ’Αγρεὺς ἀρχιε. ἀνηθ. ’Αλίοις

> Bibliography:
> L. Cesano, *Annuario*, III, p. 171, and Pl. XI, 5

Weight: 13.83 gr. (London) - 15.70 gr. (Rome)
Illustrated example: Rome

Alia 6 Plate XX

Obv.: Bust of Gordian III, l., with shield and spear
Inscription: Μ. ’Αντ. Γορδιανός Αὐγ.
Rev.: Men riding r. with axe over shoulder
Inscription: ’Αλιηνῶν

> Bibliography:
> Drexler, col. 2709
> *BMC Phrygia*, p. 45, no. 9
> *Inv. Wadd.*, *RN*, 1898, p. 390, no. 5597
> Imhoof, *Kl. M.*, I, p. 196, no. 10, and Pl. VI, no. 26 (rev. only)
> *SNG Aulock*, Pl. 110, no. 3387
> Lane, II, p. 24, Alia 5
> Kraft, Pl. 51, A and Pl. 102, 1

Weight: 6.21 gr. (London) - 9.95 gr. (Athens)
Illustrated example: Aulock

Alia 7 Plate XX

Obv.: Bust of Gordian III, r., laureate
Inscription: Αὐτ. Κ. Μ. ’Αντ. Γορδιανός
Rev.: Men riding r., axe over shoulder
Inscription: ’Αλιηνῶν

> Bibliography:
> Drexler, col. 2709 and fig. 5
> *BMC Phrygia*, p. 46 and Pl. VI, no. 7
> *Inv. Wadd.*, *RN*, 1898, p. 390 and no. 5597
> Imhoof, *Kl. M.*, I, pp. 196-7

SNG Aulock, Pl. 110, no. 3388
Lane, II, p. 25, Alia 6
Kraft, Pl. 51, no. 1 and Pl. 102, A

Weight: 8.68 gr. (Paris) - 10.50 gr. (Aulock)
Illustrated example: Aulock

Apameia 1   Plate XX

Obv.: Bust of Volusian, r., laureate
Inscription: Οὐειβ. Γάλλος Οὐολου. . . . .
Rev.: Men riding r.
Inscription: Παρ. Κλ. 'Απολιναρίου 'Απαμέων

  Bibliography:
  Engel, RN, 1884, p. 29, no. 24
  Drexler, col. 2710
  BMC Phrygia, p. 104, no. 193
  Lane, II, p. 25, Apameia 1 and Pl. VI, no. 11

Weight: 12.63 gr.-14.38 gr. (London)
Illustrated example: London

Cibyra 1   Plate XXI

Obv.: Bust of Men, r.
No inscription
Rev.: Laurel wreath containing the inscription Κιβυρατῶν

  Bibliography:
  BMC Phrygia, p. 136, no. 28
  Imhoof, Kl. M., I, p. 253, no. 17
  SNG Cop., Phrygia, Pl. VIII, no. 274
  SNG Aulock, Pl. 121, no. 3722
  Lane, II, p. 25, Cibyra 1

Weight: 2.16 gr. (Copenhagen) - 2.70 gr. (Imhoof)
Illustrated example: Aulock

Cibyra 2   Plate XXI

Obv.: Bust of Selene, r.
No inscription

Rev.: Men standing l. with staff and patera, held over flaming altar
Inscription: Κιβυρατῶν

> Bibliography:
> Weber, III, 2, p. 502, no. 7064 and Pl. 251
> Lane, II, p. 25, Cibyra 2

Weight: 3.04 gr. (London)
Illustrated example: London

Cibyra 3 Plate XXI

Obv.: Bust of Senate, r.
Inscription: Ἱερὰ Σύγκλητος
Rev.: Men standing l. with pine-cone and staff
Inscription: Κιβυρατῶν

> Bibliography:
> Drexler, col. 2714-5
> *BMC Phrygia*, p. 135, no. 27 and Pl. XVI, no. 10
> *Inv. Wadd.*, *RN*, 1898, no. 5817
> Hunt., II, p. 482, no. 2
> Lane, II, p. 25, no. 3

Weight: 3.03 gr. (Paris) - 3.65 gr. (London)
Illustrated example: London

Cibyra 4 Plate XXI

Obv.: Bust of Herakles, r.
No inscription
Rev.: Men standing l. with patera and staff, the patera held over an altar
Inscription: Κιβυρατῶν

> Bibliography:
> Drexler, col. 2715
> Imhoof-Blumer, *SNR*, 1908, p. 45, no. 4
> *SNG Fitz*, Pl. 98, no 4953
> Lane, III, p. 104, no. 7

Weight: 3.51 gr. (Imhoof) - 3.71 gr. (Cambridge)
Illustrated example: Cambridge

Cibyra 5   Plate XXI

Obv.: Bust of Gordian III, r., laureate
Inscription: Αὐ. Και. Μ. ’Αν. Γορδιανός
Rev.: Men standing l. with patera and staff. Patera is held over an altar.
Inscription: Κιβυρατῶν

> Bibliography:
> Drexler, col 2715
> *Inv. Wadd., RN*, 1898, p. 405, no. 5842
> *SNG Cop., Phrygia*, Pl. 9, no. 298
> Lane, II, Cibyra 4 and Pl. VI, no. 12

Weight: 7.14 gr. (London) - 10.33 gr. (Copenhagen)
Illustrated example: Vienna

Colossae 1   Plate XXI

Obv.: Bust of Men, r.
Inscription: Κολοσσηνῶν
Rev.: Horse (?) standing l.
Inscription: ‘Ιερω. ἀνε.

> Bibliography:
> *Inv. Wadd., RN*, 1898, p. 406, no. 5866
> Lane, II, p. 25, Colossae 1 and Pl. VI, no. 13

Weight: 2.75 gr. (Paris)
Illustrated example: Paris

Colossae 2   Plate XXI

Obv.: Bust of Caracalla, as Caesar, r.
Inscription: Αὐ. Και. Μ. Αὐ. ’Αντωνεῖνος
Rev.: Men standing l. with patera and staff, end of staff resting on bucranium
Inscription: Μενεκλῆς δὶς στεφανηφορῶν ἀνέθηκεν Κολοσσηνῶν

> Bibliography:
> *BMC Phrygia*, p. 157, no. 16, and Pl. XIX, 9 (rev. only)

Weight: 23.06 gr. (London)
Illustrated example: London

Eriza 1 Plate XXI

Obv.: Bust of Caracalla, r., laureate
Inscription: Αὐτ. Και. Μ. Αὐ. Ἀντωνεῖνος
Rev.: Men riding l. apparently bare from waist up
Inscription: Ἐριζηνῶν

> Bibliography:
> BMC Phrygia, Pl. XXVI, no. 5 and p. 202, no. 3 (rev. only)
> SNG Aulock, Pl. 116, no. 3573 and Pl. 289, no. 8362
> Lane, II, p. 25, Eriza 1

Weight: 11.53 gr. (London) - 14.82 gr. (Aulock)
Illustrated example: Aulock

Grimenothyrae 1 Plate XXI

Obv.: Bust of Senate, r.
Inscription: Ἱερὰ Σύγκλητος
Rev.: Men standing l. with pine-cone and staff
Inscription: Ἐπὶ Λ. Τυλλίου Γριμενοθυρέων (with variations)

> Bibliography:
> BMC Phrygia, p. 22, no. 1 and Pl. XXVIII, no. 1
> Inv. Wadd., RN, 1898, p. 418, no. 6056

Weight: 6.00 gr. (Paris) - 9.10 gr. (New York)
Illustrated example: London

Grimenothyrae 2 Plate XXII

Obv.: Bust of Senate, r.
Inscription: Ἱερὰ Σύγκλητος
Rev.: Men standing l. with pine-cone and staff
Inscription: Ἐπὶ Μ. Τυλλι. Γριμενοθυρέων

> Bibliography:
> Drexler, col. 2712
> BMC Phrygia, p. 223, no. 6
> Weber, III, ii, 538, no. 7191 and Pl. 257

Weight: 6.28 gr. (London) - 9.20 gr. (Weber)
Illustrated example: Istanbul

Grimenothyrae 3   Plate XXII

Obv.: Head of Herakles, r., laureate, no inscription
Rev.: Men standing l. with pine-cone and staff
Inscription: Γριμενοθυρέων

> Bibliography:
> Waddington, *RN*, 1852, p. 93, no. 1
> Drexler, col. 2712
> *Inv. Wadd.*, *RN*, 1898, p. 417, no. 6047

Weight: 2.74 gr.-3.88 gr. (Paris)
Illustrated example: Paris

Grimenothyrae 4   Plate XXII

Obv.: Bust of Caracalla, r., laureate
Inscription: Αὐτ. Μ. Αὐρ. Ἀντωνεῖνος
Rev.: Men standing l. with pine-cone and staff
Inscription: Τραιανοπολειτῶν Γρεμενοθυρέων

> Bibliography:
> Josef Scholz, *NZ*, 1910, p. 26, no. 146 and P . III, 6

Weight: 17.50 gr. (Scholz)
Illustrated example: Scholz

Hadrianopolis 1   Plate XXII

Obv.: Bust of Men, r.
Inscription: Σεβα.
Rev.: Flaming altar
Inscription: Ἀδρι.

> Bibliography:
> Imhoof, *Kl. M.*, I, p. 232, no. 2

Weight: 1.01 gr.
Illustrated example: Berlin

Hadrianopolis 2   Plate XXII

Obv.: Bust of Athena, r., with Corinthian helmet
No inscription

Rev.: Men standing l. with patera and staff
Inscription: 'Ἀδριανοπολειτῶν

> Bibliography:
> Drexler, col. 2713
> Imhoof, *Kl. M.*, I, p. 232, no. 1
> *Hunt.*, II, p. 486, Hadrianopolis 1 and Pl. LVI, no. 25
> Lane, II, p. 26, no. 2

Weight: 6.19 gr. (Glasgow)
Illustrated example: Glasgow

Hadrianopolis 3   Plate XXII

Obv.: Busts of Septimius Severus, Caracalla, and Geta, under them an eagle with spread wings
Inscription: Αὐ. Και. Λ. Σεπ. Σευ, κ. Μ. 'Αντωνει... Γέτας Κ.
Rev.: Men riding l.
Inscription: 'Ἀδριανοπολειτῶν

> Bibliography:
> *BMC Phrygia*, p. 225, no. 3 and Pl. XXVIII, 6
> Lane, II, p. 26, Hadrianopolis 1

Weight: 27.99 gr. (London)
Illustrated example: London

Hierapolis 1   Plate XXII

Obv.: Bust of Boule, r.
Inscription: Ἱερὰ Βουλή
Rev.: Men standing l. with pine-cone and staff, foot on bucranium. Crescent apparently absent.
Inscription: Ἱεραπολειτῶν

> Bibliography:
> *BMC Phrygia*, p. 243, nos. 90 and 91
> L. Weber, *NC*, 1913, p. 138, nos. 2 and 3 and Pl. III, no. 45
> Lane, II, p. 26, Hierapolis 1

Weight: 4.01 gr. (London) - 6.24 gr. (Berlin)
Illustrated example: Berlin

Hierapolis 2   Plate XXII

Obv.: Bust of Boule, l.
Inscription: Ἱερὰ Βουλή
Rev.: Men standing l. with pine-cone and staff, foot on bucranium. Crescent clear.
Inscription: Ἱεραπολειτῶν

> Bibliography:
> Grose, II, p. 244, no. 8822 and Pl. 311, no. 14
> *SNG Aulock*, Pl. 119, no. 3641

Weight: 3.50 gr. (Aulock) - 4.88 gr. (Cambridge)
Illustrated example: Cambridge

Hierapolis 3   Plate XXII

Obv.: Bust of city goddess, r.
Inscription: Νεωκόρων
Rev.: Men standing l. with pine-cone and staff, foot on bucranium
Inscription: Ἱεραπολειτῶν

> Bibliography:
> Drexler, col. 2713
> *BMC Phrygia*, p. 243, no. 92
> Weber, *NC*, 1913, p. 139, nos. 4 and 5
> *SNG Aulock*, Pl. 119, no. 3642
> Lane, II, p. 26, Hierapolis 3

Weight: 2.91 gr. (Aulock) - 4.01 gr. (London)
Illustrated example: Aulock

Hierapolis 4   Plate XXII

Obv.: Bust of Zeus Troios, r.
Inscription: Ζεὺς Τρώιος
Rev.: Men standing l. with pine-cone and staff, foot on bucranium. Crescent clear.
Inscription: Ἱεραπολειτῶν

> Bibliography:
> Von Prokesch-Osten, *Öst. Akad. der Wissenschaften, Denkschriften Phil.-Hist. Klasse*, 5, 1854, p. 292

Weight: 2.86 gr.-3.62 gr. (Berlin)
Illustrated example: Berlin

Hierapolis 5 — Plate XXIII

Obv.: Bust of Zeus Troios, r.
Inscription: Ζεὺς Τρώιος
Rev.: Men standing r. with staff and pine-cone, foot on bucranium. Crescent faintly visible.
Inscription: Ἱεραπολειτῶν Νεωκόρων

Bibliography:
Weber, III, 2, p. 516, no. 7112, and Pl. 253

Weight: 2.47 gr. (Gotha) - 5.37 gr. (Weber)
Illustrated example: Weber

Hierapolis 6 — Plate XXIII

Obv.: Bust of Faustina, jr., right
Inscription: Φαυστεῖνα Σεβαστή
Rev.: Men standing l. with pine-cone and staff. Crescent visible.
Inscription: Ἱεραπολειτῶν

Bibliography:
J. G. Milne, NC, 1940, p. 221, Hierapolis 10

Weight: 3.72 gr. (Oxford)
Illustrated example: Oxford

Hierapolis 7 — Plate XXIII

Obv.: Bust of Caracalla, r., laureate
Inscription: Αὐτ. Κ. Μ. Αὐρ. Ἀντωνεῖνος
Rev.: Men standing l. with pine-cone and staff, foot on bucranium
Inscription: Ἱεραπολειτῶν Νεωκόρων

Bibliography:
Drexler, col. 2713
BMC Phrygia, p. 252, Hierapolis, nos. 143-4
Weber, NC, 1913, nos. 6 and 7, p. 139
Lane, II, p. 26, Hierapolis 5 and Pl. VII, no. 1

Weight: 4.86 gr. (Vienna) - 5.33 gr. (London)
Illustrated example: London

Hierapolis 8 Plate XXIII

Alliance coin of Hierapolis and Ephesus
Obv.: Female bust, r.
Inscription: Ἱεραπολειτῶν κ. Ἐφεσίων
Rev.: Men standing l. with patera and staff, foot on bucranium
Inscription: Νεωκόρων Ὁμόνοια

> Bibliography:
> BMC Phrygia, p. 263, no. 187 and Pl. LII, no. 5
> Weber, JIAN, 1912, pp. 74-75, no. 6 and Pl. 10, no. 15
> Weber, III, ii, p. 517, no. 7119 and Pl. 254
> SNG Aulock, Pl. 119, no. 3663
> Lane, II, p. 26, Hierapolis 6

Weight: 3.95 gr. (Aulock) - 5.36 gr. (Vienna)
Illustrated example: Aulock
Remarks: For alliance coins of Hierapolis and Sardis see under Sardis.

Hieropolis 1 Plate XXIII

Obv.: Bust of Demos, r.
Inscription: Δῆμος
Rev.: Men standing l. with patera and staff. No bucranium. Crescent clear.
Inscription: Ἐπὶ Μ. Πωλίωνος Ἱεροπολειτῶν

> Bibliography:
> Drexler, col. 2713
> BMC Phrygia, p. 265, Hieropolis 4
> Inv. Wadd., RN, 1898, p. 426, no. 6187
> Imhoof, Kl. M., I, p. 244, no. 2
> Weber, NC, 1913, p. 139, no. 5A
> Lane, II, p. 26, Hieropolis 1 and Pl. VII, no. 2

Weight: 9.18 gr. (Paris) - 9.50 gr. (London)
Illustrated example: London
Remarks: Although the observations of L. Robert, *La Deesse de Hierapolis-Castabala*, Paris, 1964, p. 17-22, create considerable doubt as to whether the traditional numismatic distinction between Hierapolis and Hieropolis is founded on any actuality, I keep it here for the sake of convenience.

Hieropolis 2   Plate XXIII

Obv.: Bust of Demos, r.
Inscription: Δῆμος
Rev.: Men standing r. with pine-cone and staff
Inscription: Ἱεροπολειτῶν

    Bibliography: none

Weight: 5.12 gr. (Paris) - 5.84 gr. (Berlin)
Illustrated example: Paris

Hydrela 1   Plate XXIII

Obv.: Bust of Artemis, r., with bow and quiver
No inscription
Rev.: Men standing l., r. hand extended, apparently wearing long gown
Inscription: Ὑδρηλειτῶν

    Bibliography:
    BMC Phrygia, p. 271, no. 1 and Pl. XXXIII, no. 1
    Lane, II, p. 27, Hydrela 1

Weight: 3.62 gr. (London)
Illustrated example: London

Hydrela 2   Plate XXIII

Obv.: Bust of Artemis, r., with bow and quiver
No inscription
Rev.: Men riding r.
Inscription: Ὑδρη.

    Bibliography:
    SNG Aulock, Pl. 120, no. 3674
    Lane, II, p. 27, Hydrela 2

Weight: 5.00 gr. (Aulock)
Illustrated example: Aulock

Hydrela 3   Plate XXIII

Obv.:   Bust of Boule, r.
Inscription: Βουλὴ Ὑδρηλειτῶν
Rev.:   Men riding r., carrying a spear
Inscription: Ἀπελλᾶς ἀνέθηκε

> Bibliography:
> Imhoof-Blumer, *SNR*, 1913, p. 69, no. 195 and Pl. III, no. 8

Weight: 4.41 gr. (Berlin)
Illustrated example: Berlin

Hydrela 4   Plate XXIII

Obv.:   Bust of Augustus, r., bareheaded
Inscription: Σεβαστός
Rev.:   Men riding r.
Inscription: Εὐθύδωρος Ὑδρηλειτῶν

> Bibliography:
> Imhoof, *Kl. M.*, I, p. 245, Hydrela 1 and Pl. VIII, no. 3
> Lane, II, p. 27, Hydrela 3

Weight: 4.52 gr. (Berlin)
Illustrated example: Berlin

Hydrela 5   Plate XXIV

Obv.:   Bust of Nero, r., laureate
Inscription: Νέρων Σεβαστός
Rev.:   Men riding r.
Inscription: Ἀπελλᾶς Ἀθηναγόρου Ὑδρηλειτῶν

> Bibliography:
> *BMC Phrygia*, p. 272, no. 4
> Lane, II, p. 27, Hydrela 4 and Pl. VII, no. 3

Weight: 4.88 gr. (London) - 7.68 gr. (Berlin)
Illustrated example: London
Remarks: The last three coins, together with BMC Phrygia, p. 271, no. 3, and Pl. XXXIII, 2 (a coin with obv. Hadrian, rev. inscription: Ἀπελλᾶς Ἀθηναγόρου ἀνέθηκε Ὑδρηλειτῶν) present a

rather unusual situation, of which the following may be the correct explanation: Our Hydrela 2 and Hydrela 3 are stylistically very similar, therefore both seem to date from the time of Augustus. No. 2 bears the magistrate's name Apellas. He seems to have had a son, Athenagoras, and a grandson, Apellas (II). Apellas II, in the reign of Nero, not only was the magistrate who issued money, but repeats his grandfather's type. He in turn had a son, Athenagoras (II), and a grandson, Apellas (III). Apellas III in the reign of Hadrian was in turn magistrate in charge of the money, but did not choose to use the ancestral type. The periods of time elapsed between grandfathers and grandsons seem about right.

Hyrgaleis 1 Plate XXIV

Obv.: Bust of Dionysus, r.
No inscription
Rev.: Men standing l. with patera and staff
Inscription: Ὑργαλέων

> Bibliography:
> *BMC Phrygia*, p. 273, no. 2
> Lane, II, p. 27, Hyrgaleis 1 and Pl. VII, no. 4

Weight: 6.74 gr. (London)
Illustrated example: London
Remarks: The figure of Men is very poorly rendered, and only half the crescent is visible. The rendering is reminiscent of our Colossae 2.

Julia 1 Plate XXIV

Obv.: Bust of Nero, r., bareheaded
Inscription: Νέρων Καῖσαρ
Rev.: Men riding r. There is a symbol of some sort behind his shoulders.
Inscription: Σέργιος Ἡφαιστίων Ἰουλιέων

> Bibliography:
> Drexler, *NZ*, 1889, p. 183
> Drexler, col. 2714

BMC *Phrygia*, p. 276, no. 3 and Pl. XXXIII, no. 6
Imhoof, *Kl. M.*, p. 247, no. 8825, and Pl. 311, no. 15 Grose, III, p. 245, no. 8825, and Pl. 311, no. 15
SNG Cop., *Phrygia*, Pl. 14, no. 485
SNG Aulock, Pl. 120, no. 3679
Lane, II, p. 27, Julia 1

Weight: 3.42 gr. (Aulock) - 6.02 gr. (London)
Illustrated example: Aulock

Julia 2 Plate XXIV

Obv.: Bust of Nero, older than on previous coin, r., laureate
Inscription: Νέρων καῖσαρ
Rev.: Men riding r.
Inscription: Ἡφαιστίων Ἰουλιέων (?)

  Bibliography: none

Weight: 5.43 gr. (Munich)
Illustrated example: Munich

Julia 3 Plate XXIV

Obv.: Bust of Lucilla, r.
Inscription illegible
Rev.: Men standing r. with Antiochene attributes
Inscription: Ἰουλιέων

  Bibliography: none

Weight: 10.45 gr. (Paris)
Illustrated example: Paris

Julia 4 Plate XXIV

Obv.: Bust of Aemilian, r., radiate
Inscription: Αὐτ. Κ. Μ. Αἰμ. Αἰμιλιανός
Rev.: Distyle temple with statue of Men inside, standing l. with long robe, patera, staff, and foot on bucranium. Representation similar to Antiochene, but without Nike.
Inscription: ἀρχ. τὸ β' Φιλοτείμῳ Ἰουλιέων

Bibliography:
Borrell, *NC*, 1845-6, p. 29
Drexler, col. 2713-4
BMC Phrygia, p. 276, no. 4 and Pl. XXXIII, no. 7
Inv. Wadd., *RN*, 1898, p. 428, no. 6206 and Pl. XII, no. 5
SNG Aulock, Pl. 120, no. 3680
Lane, II, p. 27, Julia 2
Kraft, Pl. 52, no. 23

Weight: 13.53 gr. (London) - 15.00 gr. (Paris)
Illustrated example: Aulock

Laodiceia 1   Plate XXIV

Obv.: Bust of Men, r.
Inscription: Λαοδικέων
Rev.: Eagle on thunderbolt, head l.
Inscription: Κορ. Διοσκουρίδης

Bibliography:
Roscher, Pl. Ia, no. 6
Drexler, col. 2715
BMC Phrygia, p. 288, nos. 64-67 and Pl. XXXIV, no. 16
Inv. Wadd., *RN*, 1898, p. 429, no. 6281
Imhoof, *MG*, p. 404, no. 117
Weber, III, ii, p. 521, no. 7131, and Pl. 254
SNG Aulock, Pl. 291, no. 8411
Lane, II, p. 27, Laodiceia 1

Weight: 2.65 gr.-5.02 gr. (Paris)
Illustrated example: Aulock
Remarks: To be dated to the time of Augustus on the basis of the magistrate's name.

Laodiceia 2   Plate XXIV

Obv.: Bust of Men, r.
Inscription: Λαοδικέων
Rev.: Eagle on thunderbolt, head l.
Inscription: Κορ. Αἰνέας

Bibliography:
Imhoof, *MG*, p. 414, no. 119
Drexler, col. 2715
BMC Phrygia, p. 289, nos. 68-69

Weber, III, ii, p. 521, no. 7132 and Pl. 254
Svoronos, *JIAN*, 1911, p. 102, no. 47
Hübl, II, p. 317, no. 3568
SNG Aulock, Pl. 124, no. 3810
Lane, II, p. 27, no. 2

Weight: 3.29 gr. (London) - 4.35 gr. (Istanbul)
Illustrated example: Istanbul
Remarks: To be dated to the time of Nero on the basis of the magistrate's name.

Laodiceia 3   Plate XXIV

Obv.: Bust of Men, r.
Inscription: Λαοδικέων
Rev.: Eagle on thunderbolt, head l.
Inscription: Διονύσιος

Bibliography:
Drexler, col. 2715
BMC Phrygia, p. 293, no. 97 and Pl. XXXV, 7
Inv. Wadd., *RN*, 1898, no. 6232
Lane, II, p. 27, Laodiceia 3

Weight: 3.45 gr. (Gotha) - 6.16 gr. (London)
Illustrated example: London
Remarks: To be dated to the time of Antoninus Pius on the basis of the magistrate's name.

Laodiceia 4   Plate XXIV

Obv.: Bust of Men, r.
Inscription: Λαοδικέων
Rev.: Asklepios standing with caduceus
Inscription: Διονύσιος

Bibliography:
Imhoof, *Kl. M.*, I, p. 169, no. 31 and Pl. IX, no. 2
Lane, II, p. 27, Laodiceia 4

Weight: 5.09 gr. (Berlin)
Illustrated example: Berlin
Remarks: Likewise to be dated to the time of Antoninus Pius.

Laodiceia 5 Plate XXV

Obv.: Bust of Men, r., no inscription
Rev.: Tyche with polos standing l., altar at feet
Inscription: Λαοδικέων

> Bibliography:
> *Inv. Wadd.*, *RN*, 1898, p. 429, no. 6230
> Lane, II, p. 27, Laodiceia 5 and Pl. VII, no. 5

Weight: 6.34 gr. (Paris)
Illustrated example: Paris

Laodiceia 6 Plate XXV

Obv.: Bust of Senate, l.
Inscription: Ἱερὰ Σύγκλητος
Rev.: Men standing r. with pine-cone and staff, foot on bucranium
Inscription: Π. Κ. Ἄτταλος ἀνέθηκεν Λαοδικέων

> Bibliography:
> Imhoof, *Kl. M.*, I, p. 269, no. 34a
> Lane, II, p. 28, Laodiceia 6 and Pl. VII, 6 (rev. only)

Weight: 25.60 gr. (Berlin)
Illustrated example: Berlin
Remarks: The coin listed by Drexler, col. 2715, from Laodiceia, with obv. bust of Augustus and rev. bust of Men, as being in the Berlin collection, is not to be found there now.

Metropolis 1 Plate XXV

Obv.: Bust of Boule, r.
Inscription: Ἱερὰ Βουλή
Rev.: Men standing r. with pine-cone and bucranium. Foot on head of reclining ox. Long gown.
Inscription: Μητροπολειτῶν Φρυ.

> Bibliography:
> *BMC Phrygia*, p. 33, no. 1 and Pl. XXXIX, 1
> Imhoof, *Kl. M.*, I, p. 277, no. 2
> Lane, II, p. 28, Metropolis 1

Weight: 4.43 gr. (Berlin) - 5.06 gr. (London)
Illustrated example: London

Metropolis 2   Plate XXV

Obv.:   Bust of Boule, r.
Inscription: Βουλή
Rev.:   Men standing r. as on Metropolis 1.
Inscription: Μητροπολειτῶν Φρυ.

    Bibliography: none

Weight: 6.28 gr. (Paris)
Illustrated example: Paris

Metropolis 3   Plate XXV

Obv.:   Bust of Herennius Etruscus, r., laureate
Inscription: Αὐ. Κ. Γ. Μ. ’Ετρου. Δέκιος
Rev.:   Men striding r. with patera and staff
Inscription: Παρ. ’Αλε. Τιείου πρ. ἀρ. Μητροπολειτῶν Φρυ.

    Bibliography:
    W. M. Ramsay, *Athenische Mitteilungen*, 1882, p. 144 and *Journal of Hellenic Studies*, 1883, p. 61, no. 4
    Drexler, col. 2715
    BMC Phrygia, Metropolis 6
    Imhoof-Blumer, *Kl. M.*, I, p. 278, no. 5

Weight: 7.21 gr.-7.42 gr. (Berlin)
Illustrated example: Berlin
Remarks: The coin which Ramsay describes, from the Lawson collection, is said to have Trajan Decius on the obv., and Drexler follows Ramsay.

Midaeum 1   Plate XXV

Obv.:   Bust of Caracalla, r., laureate
Inscription: ’Αντωνεῖνος Αὐγοῦστος
Rev.:   Men standing l. with pine-cone and staff
Inscription: Μιδαέων

    Bibliography:
    BMC Phrygia, Midaeum, nos. 11 and 12

Weight: 11.24 gr. (London) - 15.71 gr. (Berlin)
Illustrated example: Berlin

COINS 71

Remarks: The Berlin example, on which the crescent is clear, confirms the identification of the London examples as Men; since the London examples lack the crescent, I had expressed doubts about the identification, Lane, II, p. 28, note 25.

Paleobeudus 1   Plate XXVI

Obv.: Bust of Hadrian, r., laureate
Inscription: Αὐ. Και. Τρα. 'Αδριανός
Rev.: Men standing l. with patera and staff
Inscription: Παλαιοβευδηνῶν

> Bibliography:
> Löbbecke, *Z. für N.*, 1887, p. 50
> Roscher, Pl. Ia, no. 11 (rev. only)
> Drexler, col. 2711
> *BMC Phrygia*, p. 346, no. 2
> Lane, II, p. 28, Palaeobeudus 1

Weight: 3.88 gr.-8.23 gr. (Berlin)
Illustrated example: Berlin

Philomelium 1   Plate XXVI

Obv.: Bust of Men, r., laureate
No inscription
Rev.: Zeus seated l. with eagle and scepter
Inscription: Φιλομηλ. Σκυθινο.

> Bibliography:
> Imhoof, *Gr. M.*, p. 743, nos. 716-717
> Drexler, col. 2717
> *BMC Phrygia*, p. 353, no. 1-2 and Pl. XLI, no. 11
> *Inv. Wadd.*, *RN*, 1898, p. 553, nos. 6394-5
> Weber, III, ii, p. 531, no. 7165 and Pl. 256
> *SNG Aulock*, Pl. 129, no. 3915
> Lane, II, p. 28, Philomelium, 1

Weight: 4.45 gr. (Aulock) - 8.98 gr. (London)
Illustrated example: Aulock

Philomelium 2 Plate XXVI

Obv.:   Bust of Augustus, r., bareheaded
Inscription: Σεβαστός
Rev.:   Bust of Men, r.
Inscription: Φιλομηλέων Φλάκκος (?)

> Bibliography:
> Lane, II, p. 28, Philomelion 2 and Pl. VII, no. 8

Weight: 3.43 gr. (New York) - 3.50 gr. (Istanbul)
Illustrated example: Istanbul

Philomelium 3 Plate XXVI

Obv.:   Bust of Tiberius, r., bareheaded
Inscription: Σεβαστός
Rev.:   Bust of Men, r.
Inscription: Φιλομηλέων Τῖτος Φιλόπατρις

> Bibliography:
> *Inv. Wadd.*, *RN*, 1898, p. 553, no. 6397
> Lane, II, p. 28, Philomelion 3 and Pl. VII, no. 9

Weight: 2.96 gr. (Vienna) - 4.01 gr. (Paris)
Illustrated example: Paris
Remarks: Titos Philopatris is a known magistrate of the time of Tiberius, and we can thus be sure that the emperor portrayed is not intended for Augustus.

Prymnessus 1 Plate XXVI

Obv.:   Bust of Men, r., with starry cap
No inscription
Rev.:   Hygeia standing r., draped, feeding snake from patera
Inscription: Πρυμνησσέων

> Bibliography:
> *BMC Phrygia*, p. 362, no. 5 and Pl. XLII. no. 8
> Lane, II, p. 28, Prymnessus 1

Weight: 3.35 gr. (London) - 3.46 gr. (Vienna)
Illustrated example: London

Prymnessus 2   Plate XXVI

Obv.: Bust of Men, r., with starry cap
No inscription
Rev.: Tyche standing l. with kalathos, rudder, and cornucopia
Inscription: Πρυμνησσέων

> Bibliography:
> BMC Phrygia, p. 361, no. 4
> Lane, II, p. 28, Prymnessus 2 and Pl. VII, no. 10

Weight: 4.60 gr. (Istanbul) - 4.77 gr. (London)
Illustrated example: Istanbul

Sebaste 1   Plate XXVI

Obv.: Bust of Men, r.
No inscription
Rev.: Hygeia standing, head l., feeding serpent from patera
Inscription: Σεβαστηνῶν

> Bibliography:
> Birch, NC, 1839-40, p. 226, fig. 2
> Drexler, col. 2717
> BMC Phrygia, p. 370, no. 8-9 and Pl. XLIII, 5
> Inv. Wadd., RN, 1898, p. 557, no. 6466 and Pl. XV, no. 10
> Lane, II, p. 28, Sebaste 1

Weight: 2.74 gr. (Vienna) - 3.24 gr. (London)
Illustrated example: Paris

Sebaste 2   Plate XXVI

Obv.: Bust of Men, r.
No inscription
Rev.: Asklepios standing frontally with caduceus
Inscription: Σεβαστηνῶν

> Bibliography:
> Drexler, Z. für N., 1887, p. 78
> Roscher, Pl. Ia, no. 9 (obv. only)
> Drexler, col. 2717
> BMC Phrygia, p. 370, no. 7
> Lane, II, p. 28, Sebaste 2 and Pl. VIII, no. 1

Weight: 3.07 gr. (London) - 4.29 gr. (Vienna)
Illustrated example: London

Sebaste 3   Plate XXVI

Obv.:   Male bust of Senate, r.
Inscription: Ἱερὰ Σύγκλητος
Rev.:   Men standing r. with pine-cone and staff, foot on bucranium
Inscription: Σεβαστηνῶν

> Bibliography:
> Drexler, col. 2717
> *BMC Phrygia*, p. 371, no. 11 and Pl. XLIII, no. 7 (rev. only)
> *SNG Aulock*, Pl. 130, no. 3949
> Lane, II, p. 28, Sebaste 3

Weight: 5.79 gr. (Paris) - 8.11 gr. (Aulock)
Illustrated example: Aulock

Sebaste 4   Plate XXVI

Obv.:   Bust of Geta, r., bareheaded
Inscription: Πο. Σεπ. Γέτας Καὶ.
Rev.:   Men standing r., with pine-cone and staff
Inscription: Σεβαστηνῶν

> Bibliography:
> Waddington, *RN*, 1851, p. 181, no. 5 and Pl. 10, 5
> Drexler, *Z. für N.*, 1887, p. 80-81
> Drexler, col. 2717
> *BMC Phrygia*, p. 375, no. 36-37
> Weber, III, ii, p. 534, no. 7177, and Pl. 256
> *SNG Cop., Phrygia*, Pl. 20, no. 682

Weight: 5.83 gr. (London) - 9.20 gr. (Copenhagen)
Illustrated example: Evelpides

Sebaste 5   Plate XXVII

Alliance coin of Sebaste and Temenothyrae
Obv.:   Facing busts of Valerian and Gallienus
Inscription: Αὐ. Κ. Πο. Λι. Οὐαλεριανός Αὐ Κ. Πο. Λικι. Γαλλιηνός

Rev.: Tyches of Sebaste and Temenothyrae standing facing each other, holding in their joined hands a statue of Men with pine-cone and staff
Inscription: Τημενοθυρέων κὲ Σεβαστηνῶν ὁμόνοια Κλεόβουλος ἄρχων

>Bibliography:
>B. de Koehne, *RBN*, 1878, p. 238, no. 4 and Pl. XX, no. 4
>*BMC Phrygia*, p. 417, no. 42 and Pl. LIII, no. 7 (rev. only)
>*Inv. Wadd.*, *RN*, 1898, p. 602, no. 7063
>Weber, III, ii, p. 540, no. 7196 and Pl. 257
>*SNG Aulock*, Pl. 132, no. 4012
>Lane, II, p. 29, Sebaste 5

Weight: 27.77 gr. (Aulock) - 32.95 gr. (Koehne)
Illustrated example: Aulock
Remarks: The identification of the small figure as Men is probably correct, although the crescent does not really seem to be clear on any example.

Siblia 1   Plate XXVII

Obv.: Bust of Men, r.
No inscription
Rev.: Telesphorus standing frontally
Inscription: Σιβλιανῶν

>Bibliography:
>Drexler, *Z. für N.*, 1887, p. 78
>Drexler, col. 2718
>Lane, II, p. 29, Siblia 2 and Pl. VIII, no. 2

Weight: 4.54 gr. (Vienna)
Illustrated example: Vienna

Siblia 2   Plate XXVII

Obv.: Bust of Augustus, r., bareheaded. Lituus in field.
Inscription: Σεβαστός
Rev.: Bust of Men, l., with starry cap
Inscription: Ἰούλιος Καλλικλῆς Σιβλιανῶν

Bibliography:
Imhoof, *Gr. M.*, p. 747, no. 737
Imhoof, *MG*, p. 411, no. 150
Drexler, col. 2718
SNG Aulock, Pl. 130, no. 3955
Lane, II, p. 29, Siblia 1

Weight: 4.91 gr. (London) - 5.35 gr. (Aulock)
Illustrated example: Aulock

Siblia 3   Plate XXVII

Obv.: Bust of Tiberius r., bareheaded
Inscription: Τιβέριος Σεβαστός
Rev.: Bust of Men, l.
Inscription: Δῆμος Σιβλιανῶν

Bibliography:
SNG Fitz., Pl. 100, no. 5005
Lane, III, p. 104-5, no. 8

Weight: 5.27 gr. (Cambridge) - 5.81 gr. (London)
Illustrated example: London

Siblia 4   Plate XXVII

Obv.: Bust of Julia Domna, r.
Inscription: Ἰουλία Δόμνα Σεβαστή
Rev.: Men (Selene?) standing r. with staff and statuette of Nike, foot on bucranium (mule's head?)
Inscription: Σειβλιανῶν

Bibliography:
Kenner, *NZ*, 1872, pp. 247-9, Pl. 10, fig. 7
Drexler, col. 2718
Lane, II, p. 29, Siblia 3 and Pl. VII, no. 3
Kraft, Pl. 79, no. 26a

Weight: 12.62 gr. (Vienna)
Illustrated example: Vienna
Remarks: For a discussion of the obviously female-looking Men (Selene?) on this and the following coin, see L. Robert, *Centennial Publication of the American Numismatic Society*, New York, 1958, p. 578. Robert is of the opinion that the divinity repre-

sented is Selene. If so, she borrows the attributes of Men of Antioch in Pisidia. For a possible reverse example, see the biga-type of Temenothyrae, where Men borrows Selene's iconography.

Siblia 5   Plate XXVII

Obv.: Bust of Caracalla, r., laureate
Inscription: Αὐτ. Και. Κ. Αὐ. 'Αντωνεῖνος
Rev.: Men (Selene?) standing r. with staff and statuette of Nike. Foot on bucranium (mule's head?)
Inscription: Σιβλιανῶν

> Bibliography:
> *SNG Aulock*, Pl. 130, no. 3956
> L. Robert, *Centennial Publication of the ANS*, p. 578
> Lane, II, p. 29, Siblia 4
> C. Vermeule, *Roman Imperial Art in Greece and Asia Minor*, 1968, p. 165, and fig. 100.
> Kraft, Pl. 82, no. 46b

Weight: 13.76 gr. (Aulock)
Illustrated example: Aulock

Synnada 1   Plate XXVII

Obv.: Bust of Sarapis, r.
No inscription
Rev.: Men standing l. with patera and staff
Inscription: Συνναδέων

> Bibliography:
> *Inv. Wadd., RN*, 1898, p. 561, no. 6524 and Pl. XN, no. 13
> Lane, II, p. 29, Synnada 1

Weight: 6.64 gr. (Paris)
Illustrated example: Paris

Synnada 2   Plate XXVII

Obv. Bust of Roma (Athena?), r.
No inscription
Rev.: Men standing l. with patera and staff
Inscription: Συνναδέων

Bibliography:
Drexler, col. 2718
Imhoof-Blumer, *SNR*, 1908, p. 56, Synnada 2

Weight: 4.13 gr. (Vienna, broken) - 5.91 gr. (Vienna)
Illustrated example: Vienna

Synnada 3   Plate XXVII

Obv.: Bust of Marcus Aurelius, r., young
Inscription: Αὐρήλιος Βῆρος Καῖσαρ
Rev.: Men standing l. with patera and staff
Inscription: Πείσωνος Τερτ. Συνναδέων

Bibliography:
Imhoof, *Gr. M.*, p. 748, no. 743
Drexler, col. 2718

Weight: 6.50 gr. (Berlin)
Illustrated example: Berlin

Temenothyrae 1   Plate XXVIII

Obv.: Bust of Senate, r.
Inscription: Ἱερὰ Σύγκλητος
Rev.: Men standing l. with pine-cone and staff
Inscription: Σκοπελιανὸς ἀνέθηκε Τημενοθυρεῦσι (with variations)

Bibliography:
Borrell, *NC*, 1845, p. 12, no. 2
Drexler, col. 2718
BMC Phrygia, p. 407, nos. 2 and 3 and Pl. XLVII, no. 7 (rev. only)
Inv. Wadd., *RN*, 1898, p. 374, nos. 5319-20
Lane, II, p. 30, Temenothyrae 1

Weight: 6.93 gr.-8.62 gr. (London)
Illustrated example: Paris

Temenothyrae 2   Plate XXVIII

Obv.: Bust of Demos, r., diademed
Inscription: Δῆμος Φλαβιοπολειτῶν
Rev.: Men standing l. with pine-cone and staff
Inscription: Πουβ. Λονγᾶς ἀρχ. α′ Τημενοθυρεῦσι

Bibliography:
Drexler, col. 2718
BMC Phrygia, Temenothyrae 8
Lane, II, p. 30, Temenothyrae 2

Weight: 14.97 gr. (London) - 16.68 gr. (Vienna)
Illustrated example: London

Temenothyrae 3   Plate XXVIII

Obv.: Bust of Men, r.
No inscription
Rev.: Athena (Roma?) standing r.
Inscription: Ἄτταλος Τημενοθυρεῦσι

Bibliography:
Inv. Wadd., *RN*, 1898, p. 373, no. 5309
Lane, II, p. 30, Temenothyrae 3 and Pl. VIII, no. 4

Weight: 4.80 gr. (Paris)
Illustrated example: Paris

Temenothyrae 4   Plate XXVIII

Obv.: Bust of Athena (Roma?), r.
No inscription
Rev.: Men standing l. with pine-cone and staff
Inscription: Τημενοθυρεῦσι

Bibliography:
Drexler, col. 2718
Inv. Wadd., *RN*, 1898, p. 373, no. 5307
Lane, II, p. 30, Temenothyrae 4 and Pl. VIII, no. 5

Weight: 3.02 gr. (Paris)
Illustrated example: Paris

Temenothyrae 5   Plate XXVIII

Obv.: Bust of Temenos, r.
Inscription: Τήμενος οἰκιστής
Rev.: Men standing l. with pine-cone and staff
Inscription: Μᾶρκος ἀρχ. α' Τημενοθυρεῦσι

Bibliography:
Borrell, NC, 1845, p. 12, no. 3
Drexler, col. 2718-9

Weight: 6.06 gr. (Paris) - 6.37 gr. (Vienna)
Illustrated example: Vienna

Temenothyrae 6 Plate XXVIII

Obv.: Bust of Temenos, r.
Inscription: Τήμενος οἰκιστής
Rev.: Men standing l. with pine-cone and staff
Inscription: 'Ατταλιαν. Τημενοθυρεῦσι

Bibliography: none

Weight: 6.13 gr. (Vienna)
Illustrated example: Vienna

Temenothyrae 7 Plate XXVIII

Obv.: Bust of Lucius Verus, r., laureate
Inscription: Αὐ. Και. Λ. Αὐρη. Οὐῆρος
Rev.: Men standing holding staff and pine-cone (?) in a wagon drawn l. by two bulls
Inscription: Ματέρνος ἀσιαρ. Τημενοθυρεῦσι

Bibliography:
SNG Aulock, Pl. 132, no. 4004
Lane, II, p. 30, Temenothyrae 5

Weight: 10.57 gr. (Aulock)
Illustrated example: Aulock
Remarks: The representation of Men on this and the following coin, as on nos. 10 and 11, is borrowed from that of Selene, as she appears on the coins of Magnesia on the Maeander and of Tarsus.

Temenothyrae 8 Plate XXIX

Obv.: Bust of Commodus, r., laureate
Inscription: Αὐ. Λ. Αὐρήλιος Κόμοδος
Rev.: Men standing holding pine-cone and staff, in biga drawn l. by two bulls

Inscription: Γ. 'Αρον. Ματέρνος ἀσιαρ. Τημενοθυρεῦσι

> Bibliography:
> Imhoof, *Gr. M.*, p. 725, no. 640
> Roscher, Pl. Ib, no. 13 (rev. only)
> Drexler, col. 2719
> *BMC Phrygia*, p. 412, no. 21 and Pl. XLVIII, no. 1
> *SNG Cop.*, *Phrygia*, Pl. 23, no. 741
> Lane, II, p. 30, Temenothyrae, no. 6

Weight: 12.88 gr. (Copenhagen) - 15.70 gr. (London)
Illustrated example: Copenhagen

Temenothyrae 9   Plate XXIX

Obv.: Bust of Septimius Severus, laureate, r.
Inscription: .... Σεουῆρος
Rev.: Men standing l. with pine-cone and staff
Inscription: Τημενοθυρεῦσι Σύμμαχος α'

> Bibliography: none

Weight: 15.13 gr. (Vienna)
Illustrated example: Vienna

Temenothyrae 10   Plate XXIX

Obv.: Bust of Valerian, r., radiate
Inscription: Αὐ. Κ. Λ. Πο. Λι. Οὐαλεριανός
Rev.: Men standing with pine-cone and staff in biga drawn left by two bulls
Inscription: Κλεόβουλος ἄρχων α' Τημενοθυρεῦσι

> Bibliography: none

Weight: 19.22 gr. (Berlin)
Illustrated example: Berlin

Temenothyrae 11   Plate XXIX

Obv.: Facing busts of Valerian and Gallienus
Inscription: Αὐ. Κ. Πο. Λι. Οὐαλεριανὸς Αὐ. Κ. Πο. Λικι. Γαλλιηνός

Rev.: Men standing with pine-cone and staff in biga drawn left by two bulls
Inscription: Κλεόβουλος ἄρχων αʹ Τημενοθυρεῦσι

> Bibliography:
> B. de Koehne, *RBN*, 1878, p. 237, no. 2 and Pl. XX, 2
> Drexler, col. 2719, and fig. 7
> *BMC Phrygia*, Temenothyrae 35-36
> *Inv. Wadd.*, *RN*, 1898, p. 374, no. 5330
> Lane, II, p. 30, Temenothyrae 7 and Pl. &VIII, no. 6

Weight: 19.12 gr. (London) - 25.39 gr. (Paris)
Illustrated example: Paris

Antioch 1   Plate XXX

Obv.: Bust of Men, r., laureate, with starry cap
No inscription
Rev.: Humped bull standing r.
Inscription: Ἀντιοχ. Εὐδη.

> Bibliography:
> Drexler, col. 2698 (these coins in general)
> Lane, II, p. 30, Antioch 1 (these coins in general)
> *BMC Caria*, p. 15, no. 5

Weight: 7.69 gr. (London)
Illustrated example: London

Antioch 2   Plate XXX

Obv.: Bust of Men, r., laureate, with starry cap
No inscription
Rev.: Humped bull standing r.
Inscription: Ἀντιοχ. Μενανδρο.

> Bibliography:
> *BMC Caria*, p. 15, no. 6 and Pl. III, no. 5
> *Inv. Wadd.*, *RN*, 1898, p. 43, no. 3569

Weight: 4.69 gr. (Paris) - 5.48 gr. (London)
Illustrated example: London

Antioch 3   Plate XXX

Obv.: Bust of Men, r., laureate, stars on cap. Eagle's head in field.
No inscription
Rev.: Humped bull standing r.
Inscription: 'Αντιοχ. 'Αγαθο.

    Bibliography:
    Imhoof, *Kl. M.*, II, p. 357, no. 2
    SNG Cop., *Pisidia*, Pl. I, no. 8

Weight: 3.39 gr. (Copenhagen)
Illustrated example: Copenhagen

Antioch 4   Plate XXX

Obv.: Bust of Men, r., laureate, with stars on cap
No inscription
Rev.: Humped bull standing r.
Inscription: 'Αντιοχ. 'Απολλο.

    Bibliography:
    SNG Cop., *Pisidia*, Pl. I, no. 9

Weight: 4.53 gr. (Copenhagen)
Illustrated example: Copenhagen

Antioch 5   Plate XXX

Obv.: Bust of Men, r., laureate, with stars on cap
No inscription
Rev.: Humped bull standing r.
Inscription: 'Αντιοχ. 'Ηριλοχο.

    Bibliography:
    Imhoof, *MG*, p. 304, no. 3
    BMC Caria, p. 15, no. 7
    Imhoof, *Kl. M.*, II, p. 357, no. 4
    SNG Cop., *Pisidia*, Pl. I, nos. 10 and 11

Weight: 4.37 gr. (Imhoof) - 6.39 gr. (London)
Illustrated example: Copenhagen

Remarks: *BMC Caria*, p. 15, no. 8, gives an example of a coin of this general type with magistrate's name illegible. Similar examples exist in almost every collection.

For reattribution of the BM examples from Antioch on the Maeander to Antioch in Pisidia see *NC*, 1914, p. 300.

Antioch 6   Plate XXX

Obv.: Bust of Men, r., laureate, with starry cap. Eagle's head in field.
No inscription
Rev.: Humped bull standing r.
Inscription: 'Αντιοχ. 'Αντιόχου

> Bibliography:
> Imhoof, *Kl. M.*, II, p. 357, no. 2a

Weight: 4.63 gr. (Imhoof)
Illustrated example: New York

Antioch 7   Plate XXX

Obv.: Bust of Men, r., laureate, with stars on cap
No inscription
Rev.: Humped bull standing r.
Inscription: 'Αντιοχ. Διονυσ.

> Bibliography:
> Imhoof, *MG*, p. 304, no. 4
> Imhoof, *Kl. M.*, II, p. 357, no. 3 and Pl. XII, no. 17

Weight: unavailable
Illustrated example: Imhoof

Antioch 8   Plate XXX

Obv.: Bust of Men, r., laureate, with starry cap. Eagle's head in field.
No inscription
Rev.: Humped bull standing r.
Inscription: 'Αντιοχ. Λυκισκ.

Bibliography:
Imhoof, *Kl. M.*, II, p. 357, no. 5 and Pl. XII, no. 18

Weight: 5.77 gr. (Imhoof)
Illustrated example: Imhoof

Antioch 9   Plate XXX

Obv.: Bust of Men, r., laureate, with starry cap
No inscription
Rev.: Humped bull standing r.
Inscription: 'Αντιοχ. Εὐγνω.

Bibliography:
Inv. Wadd., *RN*, 1898, p. 43, no. 3568

Weight: 6.79 gr. (Paris)
Illustrated example: Paris

Antioch 10   Plate XXX

Obv.: Bust of Men, r., with stars on cap, laureate
No inscription
Rev.: Humped bull, r.
Inscription: 'Αντιοχ. 'Αλεξαν.

Bibliography:
Inv. Wadd., *RN*, 1898, p. 43, no. 3570

Weight: 6.41 gr. (Paris)
Illustrated example: Paris

Antioch 11   Plate XXXI

Obv.: Bust of Men, r.
No inscription
Rev.: Humped bull, r.
Inscription: 'Αντιοχ. Θεοτιμ.

Bibliography: none

Weight: 6.28 gr. (London)
Illustrated example: London

Antioch 12 Plate XXXI

Obv.: Bust of Men, r., with stars on cap, laureate
No inscription
Rev.: Humped bull standing r. An inscription, now illegible, was around the edge of the coin, not in lines across it, as is customary with these coins.

    Bibliography:
    Inv. Wadd., *RN*, 1898, p. 43, no. 3566

Weight: 10.79 gr. (Paris)
Illustrated example: Paris
Remarks: A much larger and heavier example than others of this same general type.

Antioch 13 Plate XXXI

Obv.: Bust of Men, r., with stars on cap, laureate
No inscription
Rev.: Humped bull standing l.
Inscription: Ἡρώδης(?)

    Bibliography: none

Weight: 4.44 gr. (Paris)
Illustrated example: Paris

Antioch 14 Plate XXXI

Obv.: Bust of Men, r. laureate, with starry cap
No inscription
Rev.: Nike walking r. with palm-branch, decorated with fillets. In the field there are two six-pointed stars.
Inscription: Ἀντιοχέων . . .ευιν. . . .

    Bibliography:
    Imhoof, *Kl. M.*, II, p. 356, Antiocheia 1 and Pl. XII, 16
    Lane, II, p. 30, Antioch 2 (these coins in general)

Weight: unavailable
Illustrated example: Imhoof

Antioch 15   Plate XXXI

Obv.: Bust of Men, r., laureate, stars on cap
No inscription
Rev.: Nike walking r. with palm branch
Inscription: 'Αντιοχέων . . .κων. . .

    Bibliography:
    Inv. Wadd., RN, 1898, p. 43, no. 3567

Weight: 6.70 (Paris)
Illustrated example: Paris

Antioch 16   Plate XXXI

Obv.: Bust of Men, r., laureate, with starry cap
No inscription
Rev.: Nike walking r. with palm-branch, decorated with a crown. There is one six-pointed star in the field.
Inscription: 'Αντιοχέων Δανάου

    Bibliography:
    Imhoof-Blumer, *SNR*, 1908, pp. 28-29, Antiocheia 1 and Pl. II, 11.

Weight: 7.75 gr. (Berlin)
Illustrated example: Berlin

Antioch 17   Plate XXXI

Obv.: Bust of Men, r., laureate, with starry cap
No inscription
Rev.: Nike walking r. with palm branch, undecorated, eight-pointed star in field
Inscription: 'Αντιοχέων 'Αρτεμι.

    Bibliography:
    NC, 1905, p. 339, no. 32 and Pl. XII, 2
    Imhoof-Blumer, *SNR*, 1908, p. 29, no. 2

Weight: 8.09 gr. (London)
Illustrated example: London

Antioch 18 Plate XXXI

Obv.: Bust of Men, r.
Inscription: ANTIOCHI (with variations)
Rev.: Rooster, r.
Inscription: COLONIAE (with variations)

    Bibliography:
    Drexler, col. 2721 (these coins in general)
    BMC Lycia, p. 176, no. 3 and Pl. XXXI, no. 3
    Svoronos, *JIAN*, 1903, p. 222, no. 441 and Pl. XIV, 14
    Hill, *NC*, 1914, p. 302, no. 8
    A. Dieudonne, *RN*, 1930, p. 156, no. 8 and Pl. V, no. 12
    C. Allotte de la Fuye, *Arethuse*, 1931, p. 3 fig. 1 and P. 4, Fig. 2
    Lane, II, p. 30, Antioch 3 (these coins in general)
    Krzyzanowska, *MC*, Pl. IV, Table 8 and p. 141, Av. VII, IX, rev. 10,
        11; Pl. XXVI, Table 21 and pl. 169, Av., IX, rev. 13; Pl. XXVII,
        Table 22 and p. 170-171, Av. XV-XX, rev. 18-22

Weight: 1.02 gr.-1.64 gr. (examples known to Krzyzanowska)
Illustrated example: Evelpides
Remarks: Miss Krzyzanowska's book, which we encounter here for the first time, is an exhaustive study of all die-links and weights of the colonial coins of Antioch in Pisidia known to her. She assigns some of these coins to the period of Antoninus Pius, others to the time of Septimius Serverus, and leaves yet others undated.

Antioch 19 Plate XXXI

Obv.: Bust of Men, l.
Inscription: ANTIOCHI (with variations)
Rev.: Rooster r.
Inscription: COLONIAE (with variations)

    Bibliography:
    Hill, *NC*, 1914, p. 302, no. 7
    SNG Cop., *Pisidia*, Pl. I, no. 15
    Krzyzanowska, *MC*, Pl. IV, Table 8 and pl. 141, Av. X-XII, rev. 12,
        14; Pl. XXVI, Table 21, and pp. 168-69, Av. IV-V, rev. 5-6;
        Pl. XXVII, Table, 22 and p. 170-71, Av. XXII-XXVIII,
        rev. 23-29

Weight: 1.03 gr.-1.64 gr. (examples known to Krzyzanowska)
Illustrated example: Budapest

Antioch 20   Plate XXXI

Obv.:   Bust of Men, r.
Inscription: Antioch
Rev.:   Bull standing r.
Inscription: Antioch col

    Bibliography:
    Drexler, col. 2721
    Hunt., II, p. 515, no. 1 and Pl. LVIII, 11
    Lane, II, p. 30, Antioch 4 (these coins in general)

Weight: Not supplied
Illustrated example: Glasgow

Antioch 21   Plate XXXII

Obv.:   Bust of Men, l.
Inscription: Antioch (with variations)
Rev.:   Bull standing r.
Inscription: Antioch Col (with variations)

    Bibliography:
    SNG Cop., *Pisidia*, Pl. I, no. 14
    Krzyzanowska, *MC*, Pl. IV, Table 8 and p. 141, Av. XII, rev. 13;
        Pl. XXVI, Table 21, and p. 169, Av. IV, rev. 7

Weight: 1.20-1.41 gr. (examples known to Krzyzanowska)
Illustrated example: Copenhagen

Antioch 22   Plate XXXII

Obv.:   Bust of Men, l.
Inscription: Antioch
Rev.:   Goat standing r. with head turned back
Inscription: Colo

    Bibliography:
    SNG Aulock, Pl. 160, no. 4918
    Lane, II, p. 30, Antioch 5
    Krzyzanowska, *MC*, Pl. XXVI, Table 21 and p. 169, Av. IV, rev. 8

Weight: 1.12 gr.-1.27 gr. (examples known to Krzyzanowska)
Illustrated example: Aulock

Antioch 23   Plate XXXII

Obv.: Bust of Men, r.
Inscription: Antioch (with variations)
Rev.: Round altar decorated with garland, lit
Inscription: Colonia

> Bibliography:
> Krzyzanowska, *MC*, Pl. XXVII, Table 22 and p. 171, Av. XXX-XXXI, rev. 32-33

Weight: 1.32 gr.-1.37 gr. (examples known to Krzyzanowska)
Illustrated example: Leningrad

Antioch 24   Plate XXXII

Obv.: Bust of Antoninus Pius, r., laureate
Inscription: Antoninus Aug. Pius PP., Tr., P. Cos. IIII
Rev.: Men standing r. with bucranium and rooster at feet. In his outstretched l. hand he holds a statuette of Nike carrying a trophy. These are the Antiochene attributes, as they will be referred to from here on, and seem to have been copied from a cult-image of Men in Antioch.
Inscription: Mensis Col. Caes, Antioch.

> Bibliography:
> Drexler, col. 2722
> *BMC Lycia*, p. 177, no. 5
> Imhoof, *Kl. M.*, II, p. 359, no. 12
> *SNG Aulock*, Pl. 160, no. 4921
> Lane, II, p. 31, Antioch 7
> Krzyzanowska, *MC*, Pl. II, Table 5 and p. 137-8, Av. I, III, V, rev. 1-5, 7, 9, 11

Weight: 6.68 gr.-9.24 gr. (examples known to Krzyzanowska)
Illustrated example: Aulock

Antioch 25   Plate XXXII

Obv.: Bust of Antoninus Pius, l., laureate
Inscription: Antoninus Aug. Pius PP. Tr. P. Cos. IIII
Rev.: Men standing r. with Antiochene attributes
Inscription: Mensis Col. Caes. Antioch.

Bibliography:
Krzyzanowska, *MC*, Pl. II, Table 5, p. 137-8, Av. II, rev. 7, 8

Weight: 7.11 gr.-8.15 gr. (examples known to Krzyzanowska)
Illustrated example: Berlin

Antioch 26   Plate XXXII

Obv.: Bust of Antoninus Pius, r., laureate
Inscription: Antoninus Aug. Pius. PP. Tr. P. Cos. IIII
Rev.: Men standing r. with Antiochene attributes
Inscription: Coloniae Caes. Antioch

Bibliography:
BMC Lycia, p. 177, no. 6
Krzyzanowska, *MC*, Pl. II, Table 5 and pp. 137-8, Av. VII, rev. 14

Weight: 7.23 gr.-7.75 gr. (examples known to Krzyzanowska)
Illustrated example: London

Antioch 27   Plate XXXII

Obv.: Bust of Lucius Verus, laureate, l.
Inscription: L. Aurelius Caesar
Rev.: Men standing r. with Antiochene attributes
Inscription: Coloniae Caes. Antioch.

Bibliography:
Drexler, col. 2722
Imhoof, *Kl. M.*, II, p. 359, no. 14
Lane, II, p. 31, no. 8 and Pl. VIII, no. 7 (rev. only)
Krzyzanowska, *MC*, Pl. V, Table 10 and p. 142, Av. I, rev. 1

Weight: 4.72 gr.-5.28 gr. (examples known to Krzyzanowska)
Illustrated example: Berlin

Antioch 28   Plate XXXII

Obv.: Bust of Marcus Aurelius, r., laureate
Inscription: Antoninus Augustus (with variations)
Rev.: Bust of Men, l., crescent extended all the way under neck, starry cap
Inscription: Antio Colo. (with variations)

Bibliography:
BMC Lycia, p. 178, no. 10 and Pl. XXXI, 4 (rev. only)
SNG Aulock, Pl. 297, no. 8566
Lane, II, p. 31, Antioch 6
Krzyzanowska, MC, Pl. V, Table 9 and p. 141-2, Av. V-IX, rev. 16-22

Weight: 5.45 gr. (Aulock) - 6.91 gr. (heaviest known to Krzyzanowska)
Illustrated example: Aulock

Antioch 29   Plate XXXII

Obv.:   Bust of Marcus Aurelius, r., laureate
Inscription: Antoninus Augus
Rev.:   Men standing r. with Antiochene attributes
Inscription illegible

Bibliography:
Krzyzanowska, MC, Pl. V, Table 9, and p. 142, Av. X, rev. 26

Weight: 3.45 gr. (Warsaw)
Illustrated example: Warsaw

Antioch 30   Plate XXXII

Obv.:   Bust of Commodus, r., laureate, unbearded
Inscription: L. Aurelius Commodus (with variations)
Rev.:   Men standing r. with Antiochene attributes, rooster lacking on some dies
Inscription: Antiochiae Coloniae (with variations)

Bibliography:
BMC Lycia, p. 178, no. 14
Lane, II, p. 31, no. 9
Krzyzanowska, Pl. VI, Table 11, and p. 143, Av. II-III, rev. 3-4

Weight: 5.81 gr. (Paris) - 6.53 gr. (Brussels)
Illustrated example: Paris

Antioch 31   Plate XXXIII

Obv.:   Bust of Commodus, l., laureate, bearded
Inscription: Commodus Antoninus (with variations)

Rev.: Men standing r. with Antiochene attributes
Inscription: Antioch Coloniae (with variations)

> Bibliography:
> Drexler, col. 2722
> *BMC Lycia*, p. 179, no. 16
> *SNG Cop.*, *Pisidia*, Pl. I, no. 26
> *SNG Fitz.*, Pl. 104, no. 5120
> Krzyzanowska, *WN*, 1965, p. 135, fig. a
> Lane, III, p. 105, no. 9
> Krzyzanowska, *MC*, Pl. VII, Table 14, and p. 144-5, Av. V-IX, rev. 6-12

Weight: 4.45 gr. (Cambridge) - 6.82 gr. (heaviest known to Krzyzanowska)
Illustrated example: Copenhagen

Antioch 32 Plate XXXIII

Obv.: Bust of Commodus, l., radiate, bearded
Inscription: obscure on all examples
Rev.: Men standing r. with Antiochene attributes
Inscription: Coloneia Antiochae

> Bibliography:
> *BMC Lycia*, p. 179, no. 15
> *SNG Aulock*, Pl. 297, no. 8561
> Lane, II, p. 31, Antioch 10 and Pl. VIII, no. 8
> Krzyzanowska, *MC*, Pl. VII, Table 14, and p. 145, Av. X, rev. 12

Weight: 5.74 gr. (London) - 5.80 gr. (Aulock)
Illustrated example: Aulock

Antioch 33 Plate XXXIII

Obv.: Bust of Pescennius Niger, l., radiate
Inscription: Pescen....
Rev.: Men standing r. with Antiochene attributes
Inscription: Antioch Coloniae

> Bibliography:
> Lane, II, p. 31, Antioch 11

Weight: 4.35 gr. (New York)
Illustrated example: New York

Antioch 34   Plate XXXIII

Obv.:   Bust of Septimius Severus, r., laureate
Inscription: Imp. Caes. L. Sep. Severus Per. Aug. (with variations)
Rev.:   Men standing r., with Antiochene attributes, l. elbow resting on column, Nike on globe held in l. hand. (This detail of representation continues on other large denomination coins down to Gordian III)
Inscription: Col. Caes. Antioch S. R.

> Bibliography:
> *Torino, Monete Greche*, p. 303, no. 4313
> Roscher, Pl. Ia, no. 12 (rev. only)
> Drexler, col. 2722
> *BMC Lycia*, pp. 179-180, nos. 20-21 and Pl. XXXI, no. 6 (rev. only)
> *Inv. Wadd.*, *RN*, 1898, p. 44, no. 3587; p. 610, no. 7154
> *Hunt.*, II, p. 515, no. 2
> Grose, III, p. 266, nos. 8934-36 and Pl. 318, no. 6
> *SNG Cop.*, *Phrygia*, Pl. I, no. 27
> *SNG Aulock*, Pl. 161, no. 4924
> *SNG Fitz*, Pl. CIV, no. 5121
> Krzyzanowska, *WN*, 1965, Plates X-XI, XII, *passim*
> Lane, II, p. 31, Antioch 12, and III, p. 105, no. 10
> Krzyzanowska, *MC*, Pl. XIX-XX, Table 18, and p. 160-62, Av. XXXI, XXXIV-XXXVI, XXXIX, rev. 37-40, 49-56, 60

Weight: 21.33 gr.-31.38 gr. (examples known to Krzyzanowska)
Illustrated example: Aulock
Remarks: This is an abundant issue of coins, probably the most abundant of all coins with representation of Men. It appears in sales-catalogues frequently, and if they were to be listed, the bibliography would be increased immeasurably. Krzyzanowska views these large issues of the Severan dynasty at Antioch as replacing the smaller issues after a monetary reform.

Antioch 35   Plate XXXIII

Obv.:   Bust of Septimius Severus, l., laureate
Inscription: L. Sept. Se. Pert. Aug. (with variations)
Rev.:   Men standing r. with Antiochene attributes (there are variations in detail)
Inscription: Antioch. Coloniae (with variations)

Bibliography:
BMC Lycia, P. 180, no. 22
SNG Aulock, Pl. 161, no. 4927
Krzyzanowska, *WN*, 1965, Pl. I, II, VI, *passim* (these coins in general)
Lane, II, p. 31, no. 13
Krzyzanowska, *MC*, Pl. VIII-IX, Table 15, and pp. 145-47, Av. I-VIII, rev. 1-7

Weight: 4.40 gr.-7.55 gr. (examples known to Krzyzanowska)
Illustrated example: Aulock

Antioch 36   Plate XXXIII

Obv.: Bust of Septimius Severus, r., laureate
Inscription: Imp. L. Sev. Pert. Au. XVIIII (with variations)
Rev.: Men standing r. with Antiochene attributes
Inscription: Antioch. Coloniae

Bibliography:
Imhoof, *Kl. M.*, II, p. 360, no. 15
Krzyzanowska, *MC*, Pl. VII-IX, Table 15, p. 145-147, Av. VIII, rev. 8

Weight: 5.31 gr. (Vienna)
Illustrated example: Vienna
Remarks: On his copy Imhoof-Blumer reads XVIIII, but on the Vienna copy Krzyzanowska reads IIII. If Imhoof is right (something which I have been unable to check), then it destroys all of Krzyzanowska's dating.

Antioch 37   Plate XXXIII

Obv.: Bust of Septimius Severus, l., laureate
Inscription: Imp. Caes. Sep. Sev. Per. A.
Rev.: Men standing r. with Antiochene attributes
Inscription: Antioch Mensis

Bibliography:
Krzyzanowska, *MC*, Pl. VIII-IX, Table 15, pp. 145-7, Av. XIX, rev. 25-26

Weight: 4.72 gr. (Berlin) - 5.70 gr. (Vienna)
Illustrated example: Vienna

Antioch 38　　　　　　　　　　　　　　　　　　　　　Plate XXXIII

Obv.:　Bust of Septimius Severus, r., laureate
Inscription:　Imp. Caes. Sep. Sev. Perx.
Rev.:　Men standing r. with Antiochene attributes
Inscription:　Antioch Mesis Col. Ca.

>Bibliography:
>Krzyzanowska, *MC*, Pl. VIII-IX, Table 15, p. 145-7, Av. XI, rev. 13

Weight:　6.34 gr. (Berlin)
Illustrated example:　Berlin

Antioch 39　　　　　　　　　　　　　　　　　　　　　Plate XXXIII

Obv.:　Bust of Septimius Severus, r., laureate
Inscription:　Imp. P. L. Sept. Sev. Sug
Rev.:　Men standing r. with Antiochene attributes
Inscription:　Col. MHNI Antioc

>Bibliography:
>Krzyzanowska, *MC*, p. XIV, Table 17 and p. 153-4, Av. XXV, rev. 46

Weight:　4.40 gr. (Warsaw) - 5.03 gr. (Gotha)
Illustrated example:　Warsaw
Remarks:　What I have obviously done with these last coins is to separate those which portray the emperor r. from those which portray him l., and then to single out some which have particularly unusual reverse inscriptions.

Antioch 40　　　　　　　　　　　　　　　　　　　　　Plate XXXIII

Obv.:　Bust of Septimius Severus, r., radiate
Inscription:　Imp. Sep. Sev. Pert. Aug.
Rev.:　Men standing r. with Antiochene attributes
Inscription:　Antioch Coloniae Caes. (with variations)

>Bibliography:
>Krzyzanowska, *MC*, Pl. VIII-IX, Table 15, p. 145-7, Av. XII, XVII, XVIII, rev. 15-17, 23-24

Weight:　4.25 gr.-5.73 gr. (examples known to Krzyzanowska)
Illustrated example:　Athens

Antioch 41   Plate XXXIV

Obv.: Bust of Septimius Severus, r., laureate
Inscription: Imp. C. Sev. Pert. Aug.
Rev.: Bust of Men, r., with starry cap
Inscription: Antioch Coloniae

    Bibliography:
    Krzyzanowska, *WN*, 1965, Pl. I, obv. VII, rev. 10
    Krzyzanowska, *MC*, Pl. VIII, Table 15 and p. 146, Av. IX, rev. 10

Weight: 6.30 gr. (Berlin)
Illustrated example: Berlin

Antioch 42   Plate XXXIV

Obv.: Bust of Julia Domna, r.
Inscription: Iulia Augusta
Rev.: Men standing r. with Antiochene attributes
Inscription: Col. Caes. Antioch S R

    Bibliography:
    Drexler, col. 2722
    BMC Lycia, p. 181, nos. 31-32 and Pl. XXXI, 8 (rev. only)
    Inv. Wadd., *RN*, 1898, p. 44, no. 3589
    SNG Cop., *Pisidia*, Pl. 2, no. 34
    SNG Aulock, Pl. 161, no. 4928
    Krzyzanowska, *WN*, 1965, Pl. XI-XII, *passim*
    Lane, II, pp. 31-32, no. 14
    Krzyzanowska, *MC*, Pl. XXI, Table 18, and pp. 162-3, Av. XXI,
        XXII, rev. 48-52, 54, Sept. Sev. 38, 49-51, 55

Weight: 21.70 gr.-28.81 gr. (examples known to Krzyzanowska)
Illustrated example: Aulock

Antioch 43   Plate XXXIV

Obv.: Bust of Julia Domna, r.
Inscription: Iulia Domna Aug. (with variations)
Rev.: Men standing r. with Antiochene attributes
Inscription: Antioch Coloniae Caes. (with variations)

    Bibliography:
    Krzyzanowska, *WN*, 1965, Pl. II-III, *passim*. (These coins in general)

Krzyzanowska, *MC*, Pl. X, Table 15, pp. 147-49, Av. III-VII, rev. 7, 8, 11, 13, 16

Weight: 3.94 gr.-6.89 gr. (examples known to Krzyzanowska)
Illustrated example: Leningrad

Antioch 44   Plate XXXIV

Obv.: Bust of Julia Domna, r.
Inscription: Iulia Domna Aug. (with variations)
Rev.: Men standing r. with Antiochene attributes
Inscription: Antioch. Mencis Co. (with variations)

Bibliography:
Drexler, col. 2722
BMC Lycia, p. 181, no. 33
SNG Cop., Pl. 2, no. 39
SNG Aulock, Pl. 161, no. 4929
Lane, II, p. 32, no. 15
Krzyzanowska, *MC*, Pl. X, Table 15; Pl. XV-XVI, Table 17; pp. 147-49 and pp. 154-57, Av. I, II, IV, XIII, XIV, XVII, rev. 1-3, 5, 10, 25, 30, 36

Weight: 3.98 gr.-6.06 gr. (examples known to Krzyzanowska)
Illustrated example: Budapest

Antioch 45   Plate XXXIV

Obv.: Bust of Caracalla, r., laureate
Inscription: Imp. Caes. M. Aur. Antoninus Aug. (with variations)
Rev.: Men standing r. with Antiochene attributes
Inscription: Col. Caes. Antioch. S R

Bibliography:
Drexler, col. 2722
BMC Lycia, p. 182, no. 38
Hunt., II, p. 516, no. 10 (attributed to Elagabalus)
SNG Aulock, Pl. 161, no. 4933
SNG Fitz., Pl. 104, no. 5126
Krzyzanowska, *WN*, 1965, Pl. X-XIII, *passim*.
Lane, II, p. 32, no. 16
Krzyzanowska, *MC*, Pl. XXII, Table 18, and P. 163-4, Av. XXIII, XXVII, rev. 45, Sept. Sev. 37, 39, 54
Kraft, Pl. 85, no. 5

Weight: 23.15 gr.-28.65 gr. (examples known to Krzyzanowska)
Illustrated example: Glasgow

COINS 99

Antioch 46   Plate XXXIV

Obv.:   Bust of Caracalla, r., laureate
Inscription: Imp. Caes. M. Aur. An. (with variations)
Rev.:   Men standing r. with Antiochene attributes
Inscription: Antioch Coloniae Cae. (with variations)

> Bibliography:
> *SNG Fitz.*, Pl. 104, no. 5129
> Krzyzamowska, *MN*, 1965, Pl. IV, *passim* (these coins in general)
> Krzyzanowska, *MC*, Pl. XI, Table 15, and pp. 149-151, Av. I, V, VI, rev. Sept. Sev. 23, Jul. Dom. 7, 11, 16

Weight: 3.80 gr.-5.37 gr. (examples known to Krzyzanowska)
Illustrated example: Cambridge

Antioch 47   Plate XXXIV

Obv.:   Bust of Caracalla, r., laureate
Inscription: Antoninus Pius Aug. (with variations)
Rev.:   Men standing r. with Antiochene attributes
Inscription: Antioch. Col. Men. (with variations)

> Bibliography:
> *BMC Lycia*, p. 182, no. 39
> *SNG Cop.*, *Pisidia*, Pl. 2, no. 43
> Lane, II, p. 32, no. 17
> Krzyzanowska, *MC*, Pl. XI, Table 15 and Pl. XVI, XVII, Table 17, pp. 149-151 and 157-9, Av. II, VI, IX, X, rev. 4, 13, 16, 17 Jul. Dom. 10

Weight: 4.52 gr.-6.55 gr. (examples known to Krzyzanowska)
Illustrated example: Copenhagen

Antioch 48   Plate XXXIV

Obv.:   Bust of Caracalla, r., laureate
Inscription: Imp. Aur. Antoninus
Rev.:   Men standing r. with Antiochene attributes
Inscription: Fortuna Col. Antioch

> Bibliography:
> Krzyzanowska, *MC*, Pl. XI, Table 15, and pp. 149-151, Av. VIII, rev. 15

Weight: 5.60 gr. (Vienna)
Illustrated example: Vienna

Antioch 49   Plate XXXIV

Obv.:   Bust of Geta, r., laureate
Inscription: Imp. Caes. P. Sep. Getae Aug.
Rev.:   Men standing r. with Antiochene attributes
Inscription: Col. Caes. Antioch S R

>Bibliography:
>Drexler, col. 2722
>*BMC Lycia*, p. 185, no. 54
>*Hunt.*, II, p. 516, nos. 8 and 9
>*SNG Aulock*, Pl. 161, no. 4942; Pl. 297, no. 8568
>Krzyzanowska, *WN*, 1965, Pl. XI-XIV, *passim*
>Lane, II, p. 32, no. 18
>Krzyzanowska, *MC*, Pl. XXIII, Table 18, and p. 164-5, Av. XVI, rev. 23, Sept. Sev. 55, 56, Jul. Dom. 54
>Kraft, Pl. 85, no. 6

Weight: 21.80 gr. (Missouri) - 25.29 gr. (heaviest known to Krzyzanowska)
Illustrated example: Missouri

Antioch 50   Plate XXXIV

Obv.:   Bust of Geta, r., laureate
Inscription: P. Sepimios Geta
Rev.:   Men standing r. with Antiochene attributes
Inscription: Coloni. Antiochiae

>Bibliography:
>*BMC Lycia*, p. 185, no. 55
>Krzyzanowska, *MC*, Pl. XII, table 15, and p. 151, Av. II, rev. 1

Weight: 4.97 gr. (copy in author's possession) - 5.40 gr. (London)
Illustrated example: author's copy

Antioch 51   Plate XXXV

Obv.:   Bust of Geta, r., laureate
Inscription: P. Sepimios Geta

Rev.: Men standing r. with Antiochene attributes
Inscription: Antioch Mencis Col.

    Bibliography:
    Krzyzanowska, *MC*, Pl. XII, Table 15, and p. 151, Av. II, rev. 2

Weight: 4.95 gr. (Vienna)
Illustrated example: Vienna

Antioch 52   Plate XXXV

Obv.: Bust of Geta, r., laureate
Inscription: Imp. Caes. P. Sep. Getae Aug.
Rev.: Men standing r. with Antiochene attributes, as on other coins of the larger denomination, except that in his extended hand he holds not a figure of Nike, but a band with two loops under his arm, one above
Inscription: Col. Caes. Antioch S

    Bibliography:
    Krzyzanowska, *WN*, 1965, 1965, Pl. XIV, rev. die 37
    Lane, II, p. 32, no. 24, and Pl. IX, 4
    Krzyzanowska, *MC*, Pl. XXIII, Table 18, Av. XVI, rev. 24

Weight: 23.80 gr. (Vienna)
Illustrated example: Vienna

Antioch 53   Plate XXXV

Obv.: Bust of Elagabalus, r., laureate
Inscription: Imp. C. M. Aurel. Antoninus Pius Aug.
Rev.: Men standing r. with Antiochene attributes
Inscription: Col. Caes. Antioch S R

    Bibliography:
    BMC Lycia, p. 182, no. 37 (attributed to Caracalla)
    Krzyzanowska, *MC*, Pl. XXVIII Table 23, and p. 171-2, Av. I, rev. 1

Weight: 23.91 gr.-25.73 gr. (London)
Illustrated example: London

Antioch 54 Plate XXXV

Obv.: Bust of Gordian III, r., laureate
Inscription: Imp. Caes. M. Ant. Gordianus Aug. (with variations in arrangement)
Rev.: Men standing r. with Antiochene attributes
Inscription: Col. Caes. Antioch S R (with variations in arrangement)

> Bibliography:
> Drexler, col. 2722
> *Hunt.*, II, p. 516, no. 13
> J. Scholz, *NZ*, 1901, p. 40, no. 71 and Pl. VII (rev. only)
> Dieudonne, *RN*, 1902, p. 347, no. 87 and Pl. X, 7
> Grose, II, p. 268, no. 8947 and Pl. 319, 7
> Krzyzanowska, *WN*, 1964, Pl. I, VI, VIII, IX, *passim*.
> Lane, II, p. 32, no. 19
> Krzyzanowska, *MC*, Pl. XXI-XXXIX, Table 27 and p. 175-185, Av. IV, XII, XX, XXII, rev. 13, 14, 60, 82, 94

Weight: 24.17 gr. (Scholz) - 27.56 gr. (heaviest known to Krzyzanowska)
Illustrated example: Paris

Antioch 55 Plate XXXV

Obv.: Bust of Gordian III, r., laureate
Inscription: Imp. Caes. M. Ant. Gordianus Aug.
Rev.: Bust of Men, r., with starry cap
Inscription: Col. Ces. Antioci SR (with variations)

> Bibliography:
> *Inv. Wadd.*, *RN*, 1898, p. 45, no. 3601
> L. Cesano, *Annuario*, 1916-20, p. 170, and Pl. XI, 4
> Krzyzanowska, *WN*, 1964, Pl. XI, no. § 1
> Lane, II, p. 32, no. 20 and Pl. VIII, no. 10
> Krzyzanowska, *MC*, Pl. XXXI, XXXIX, Table 27 and p. 185, Av. XXIX, rev. 107-108

Weight: 6.12 gr.-6.80 gr. (examples known to Krzyzanowska)
Illustrated example: Paris

Antioch 56   Plate XXXVI

Obv.:   Bust of Gordian III, r., laureate
Inscription: Imp. Caes. M. Ant. Gordianus Au. (with variations)
Rev.:   Men with Antiochene attributes standing in a temple, barrier in front of temple
Inscription: Caes. Antioch. Col. S R

> Bibliography:
> Imhoof, *Kl. M.*, p. 361, no. 23
> Krzyzanowska, *WN*, 1964, Pl. VIII, *passim*.
> Lane, II, p. 32, no. 20a
> Krzyzanowska, *MC*, Pl. XXXI, XXXIX, Table 27, p. 182-3, Av. XVIII-XIX, rev. 81

Weight: 21.67 gr.-25.63 gr. (examples known to Krzyzanowska)
Illustrated example: London

Antioch 57   Plate XXXVI

Obv.:   Bust of Gordian III, r., laureate
Inscription: Imp. Caes. M. Ant. Gordianus Au.
Rev.:   Men with Antiochene attributes standing on a pedestal at l. of coin, extending his hand to Tyche who stands on a pedestal on the r. side of coin. Between them there is an altar.
Inscription: Caes. Antioch Col. S R

> Bibliography:
> Drexler, col. 2722
> Krzyzanowska, *WN*, 1964, Pl. X, no. 8 (with obv. type XXI)
> Lane, II, p. 32, no. 25 and Pl. IX, no. 5
> Krzyzanowska, *MC*, Pl. XXXI-XXXIX, Table 27, and p. 183, Av. XXX, XXIII, rev. 89-97

Weight: 21.95 gr.-25.06 gr. (examples known to Krzyzanowska)
Illustrated example: Vienna

Antioch 58   Plate XXXVI

Obv.:   Bust of Philip I, r., radiate
Inscription: Imp. M. Iul. Philippus A.
Rev.:   Men standing r. with Antiochene attributes
Inscription: Antiochi Col. S R (with variations)

Bibliography:
Drexler, col. 2722
BMC Lycia, p. 195, no. 109
Lane, II, p. 32, no. 21 and Pl. IX, no. 1
Krzyzanowska, *MC*, Pl. XLII-XLIII, Table 29, and p. 191, Av. IX, rev. 30, Phil II, 29

Weight: 7.07 gr. (lightest known to Krzyzanowska) - 10.42 gr. (Oxford)
Illustrated example: Oxford

Antioch 59   Plate XXXVI

Obv.: Bust of Philip II, r., radiate
Inscription: Imp. M. Iul. Philippus Aug.
Rev.: Men standing r. with Antiochene attributes
Inscription: Antiochi Colon S R

Bibliography:
Lane, II, p. 32, no. 22 and Pl. IX, no. 2
Krzyzanowska, *MC*, Pl. XL-LXI, Table 28 and p. 188, Av. III, rev. 29

Weight: 8.03 gr.-9.73 gr. (examples known to Krzyzanowska)
Illustrated example: Berlin

Antioch 60   Plate XXXVI

Obv.: Bust of Volusian, r., radiate
Inscription: Imp. C. Vimp. Galussiano Aug.
Rev.: Men standing l. with Antiochene attributes (including the globe and column which characterize the large-denomination coins from Septimius Serverus to Gordian III)
Inscription: Antiochicla S R

Bibliography:
Lane, II, p. 32, no. 23, and Pl. IX, 3
Krzyzanowska, *MC*, Pl. LXV-XLVI, Table 32 and p. 196, Av. VI, rev. 19

Weight: 5.86 gr. (Budapest) - 9.38 gr. (heaviest known to Krzyzanowska)
Illustrated example: Budapest

Apollonia Pisidiae 1 Plate XXXVI

Obv.: Bust of Men
No inscription
Rev.: Quiver(?)
Inscription: Ἀπολλωνιατῶν

  Bibliography: none

Weight: 2.10 gr. (Paris)
Illustrated example: Paris

Apollonia Pisidiae 2 Plate XXXVI

Obv.: Bust of Marcus Aurelius, l., bareheaded
Inscription: Αὐρηλ. Και.
Rev.: Men standing l. with a bunch of grapes
Inscription: Ἀπολλωνι. Λυκ.

  Bibliography:
  Waddington, *RN*, 1853, p. 180 f., no. 4
  Drexler, col. 2722-2723
  Inv. Wadd., *RN*, 1898, p. 46, no. 3623, and Pl. III, 5 (rev. only)
  Imhoof-Blumer, *SNR*, 1913, p. 85, no. 242
  Lane, II, p. 33, Apollonia 1

Weight: 5.74 gr. (Paris) - 6.26 gr. (Berlin)
Illustrated example: Paris

Ariassus 1 Plate XXXVII

Obv.: Bust of Caracalla, r., laureate
Inscription: Αὐ. Κ. Μ. Αὐ. Ἀντωνεῖνος
Rev.: Men riding l.
Inscription: Ἀριασσέων

  Bibliography:
  B. Biondelli, *Instituto Lombardo, Rendiconti*, 1883, p. 80, no. 100
  Drexler, col. 2723
  Lane, III, Pl. XXV, no. 1
  Münzen und Medaillen, Auktion 41, 18-19 June 1970, p. 66, and
    Pl. 31, no. 516

Weight: 18.90 gr. (M & M), 38.10 gr. (Milan)
Illustrated example: Milan

Baris 1   Plate XXXVII

Obv.:   Bust of Gordian III, r., with diadem
Inscription: Αὐ. Γορδιανὸς ’Α.
Rev.:   Men standing r. with pine-cone, bucranium at feet
Inscription: Βαρηνῶν

    Bibliography:
    Imhoof-Blumer, *SNR*, 1908, p. 72, Baris 1

Weight: 4.84 gr. (Berlin)
Illustrated example: Berlin

Baris 2   Plate XXXVII

Obv.:   Bust of Trajan Decius, r., laureate
Inscription: Αὐτ. Γ. Μ. Κ. Τραιανὸς Δέκιος Σβ.
Rev.:   Men riding r.
Inscription: Βαρηνῶν

    Bibliography:
    Inv. Wadd., *RN*, 1898, p. 48, no. 3647
    SNG Cop., *Pisidia*, Pl. 5, no. 111
    SNG Aulock, Pl. 165, no. 5014
    Kraft, Pl. 52, no. 27

Weight: 6.64 gr. (Aulock) - 7.85 gr. (Copenhagen)
Illustrated example: Aulock

Baris 3   Plate XXXVII

Obv.:   Bust of Herennius Etruscus, r., bareheaded
Inscription: Γ. Μ. Κ. ’Ετρουσκ. Δέκιος Κ.
Rev.:   Men standing l. with pine-cone (?) and bucranium
Inscription: Βαρηνῶν

    Bibliography:
    Wroth, *NC*, 1898, p. 117, no. 33
    Grose, III, p. 273, no. 8975, and Pl. 321, 10
    Lane, II, p. 33, Baris 3

Weight: 6.12 gr. (Cambridge) - 7.41 gr. (London)
Illustrated example: Cambridge

Baris 4   Plate XXXVII

Obv.: Bust of Herennius Etruscus, r., bareheaded
Inscription: Γ. Μ. Κ. 'Ετρουσκ. Δέκιος Κ.
Rev.: Men riding r.
Inscription: Βαρηνῶν

> Bibliography:
> Borrell, *NC*, 1847, p. 93, no. 2
> Cavedoni, *Annali dell' Instituto*, 1861, p. 48
> Drexler, col. 2723
> Lane, II, p. 33, note 30

Weight: 6.07 gr. (Paris)
Illustrated example: Paris

Baris 5   Plate XXXVII

Obv.: Bust of Hostilian, r., bareheaded
Inscription: Μέσσιος Κυίντος Κ.
Rev.: Men standing l. with pine-cone, foot on bucranium
Inscription: Βαρηνῶν

> Bibliography:
> Imhoof, *Kl. M.*, II, p. 367, no. 9
> *SNG Fitz.*, Pl. 105, no. 5160
> Lane, III, p. 105, no. 13

Weight: 3.95 gr. (Cambridge)
Illustrated example: Cambridge

Baris 6   Plate XXXVII

Obv.: Bust of Trebonianus Gallus, r., laureate
Inscription: Αὐτ. Γ. Οὐειβ. Τρβ. Γαλλο. Σεβ. (with variations)
Rev.: Men standing l. with pine-cone, no bucranium
Inscription: Βαρηνῶν

> Bibliography:
> Borrell, *NC*, 1847, p. 93, no. 3
> *Inv. Wadd.*, *RN*, 1898, p. 48, no. 3651
> Weber, III, ii, p. 592, no. 7383 and Pl. 265
> *SNG Fitz*, Pl. 105, no. 5161
> Lane, III, p. 105, no. 14; II, p. 33, Baris 4

Weight: 5.88 gr. (Paris) - 7.38 gr. (London)
Illustrated example: Cambridge

Baris 7   Plate XXXVII

Obv.:   Bust of Volusian, r., laureate
Inscription: Οὐειβ. Γάλλος Οὐολλούσσιος Σ. (with variations)
Rev.:   Men standing l. with pine-cone and bucranium
Inscription: Βαρηνῶν

> Bibliography:
> Löbbecke, *Z. für N.*, 1885, p. 327
> Wroth, *NC*, 1894, p. 15, no. 18
> Drexler, col. 2723
> *BMC Lycia*, p. 209, no. 11 and Pl. XXXIV, 5 (rev. only)
> *Inv. Wadd.*, *RN*, 1898, p. 48, no. 3655
> *SNG Cop.*, *Pisidia*, Pl. 5, no. 116
> Lane, II, p. 33, Baris 2 and 5, and Pl. IX, 6

Weight: 5.74 gr. (Copenhagen) - 7.55 gr. (Istanbul)
Illustrated example: Istanbul

Colbasa 1   Plate XXXVII

Obv.:   Bust of Antoninus Pius, r., laureate
Inscription: Αὐ. Καῖσαρ 'Αντωνεῖνος
Rev.:   Men standing l. with patera and bucranium
Inscription: Κολβασέων

> Bibliography:
> Wroth, *NC*, 1900, p. 22, no. 26
> Lane, II, p. 33, Colbasa 1 and Pl. 14, no. 7
> Aulock, *J. N. u. G.*, 1969, p. 81 and Pl. 6, no. 1

Weight: 3.13 gr.-4.21 gr. (examples known to Aulock)
Illustrated example: London

Colbasa 2   Plate XXXVIII

Obv.:   Bust of Caracalla, r., laureate
Inscription: Αὐ. Κ. Μ. Αὐ. 'Αντωνεῖνος
Rev.:   Men standing l. with pine-cone and bucranium
Inscription: Κολβασέων

Bibliography:
Imhoof-Blumer, *SNR*, 1908, p. 76, Kolbasa 1
SNG Aulock, Pl. 166, no. 5061
Lane, II, p. 54, Colbasa 2
Aulock, *J. N. u. G.*, 1969, p. 82, and Pl. 6, no. 5

Weight: 3.88 gr.-4.60 gr. (examples known to Aulock)
Illustrated example: Aulock

Conana 1   Plate XXXVIII

Obv.: Bust of Hadrian, r., laureate
Inscription: Αὐ. Τρα. ᾽Αδριανός
Rev.: Men standing l. with pine-cone
Inscription: Κονανέων

Bibliography:
Borrell, *NC*, 1847, p. 94, no. 1
Drexler, col. 2723
BMC Lycia, p. 213, no. 2 and Pl. XXXIV, 13 (rev. only)
Inv. Wadd., *RN*, 1898, p. 50, no. 3680
Lane, II, p. 34, Conana 1

Weight: 2.83 gr. (Paris) - 3.40 gr. (London)
Illustrated example: Paris

Conana 2   Plate XXXVIII

Obv.: Bust of Marcus Aurelius, l. laureate
Inscription: Αὐτ. Καῖσαρ ᾽Αντωνεῖνος
Rev.: Men standing l. with pine-cone
Inscription: Κονανέων

Bibliography:
Drexler, col. 2723
Imhoof, *Kl. M.*, II, p. 381, Konana 3
Lane, II, p. 34, Conana 2 and 4 and Pl. IX, 8 and 9

Weight: 8.36 gr. (Vienna) - 11.24 gr. (Leningrad)
Illustrated example: Leningrad

Conana 3   Plate XXXVIII

Obv.: Bust of Caracalla, r., laureate
Inscription: Αὐτ. Και. Μ. Αὐ. ᾽Αντωνεῖνος

Rev.: Men standing l. with pine-cone
Inscription: Κονανέων

>Bibliography:
>SNG *Aulock*, Pl. 167, no. 5070
>Lane, II, p. 34, Conana 5

Weight: 11.61 gr. (Aulock)
Illustrated example: Aulock

Conana 4   Plate XXXVIII

Obv.: Bust of Severus Alexander, r., laureate
Inscription: Αὐτ. Κ. Μ. Αὐ. Σε. ᾽Αλέξανδρος Σε.
Rev.: Men standing l. with patera over altar. The end of his staff is decorated with a crescent.
Inscription: Κονανέων

>Bibliography:
>Drexler, col. 2723
>Imhoof, *Kl. M.*, II, p. 381, Konana 4 and Pl. XIII, 21 (rev. only)
>Lane, II, p. 34, Conana 3

Weight: 12.88 gr. (Berlin)
Illustrated example: Berlin

Lysinia 1   Plate XXXVIII

Obv.: Bust of Geta, r., bareheaded
Inscription: Π. Σεπ. Γέτας Κ.
Rev.: Men standing r. with Antiochene attributes, but without rooster
Inscription: Λυσινιέων

>Bibliography:
>Babelon, *RN*, 1983, p. 340, no. 37, and Pl. IX, no. 19 (rev. only)
>Drexler, col. 2723-24, fig. 8
>Wroth, *NC*, 1902, p. 341, no. 38, and Pl. XVII, no. 6
>SNG *Cop.*, *Pisidia*, Pl. VI, no. 168
>SNG *Aulock*, Pl. 169, no. 5124; Pl. 299, no. 8611
>Lane, II, p. 34, Lysinia 1

Weight: 5.17 gr.-7.60 gr. (Aulock)
Illustrated example: Aulock

Olbasa 1 Plate XXXVIII

Obv.:   Bust of Antoninus Pius, r., laureate
Inscription: Imp. Ant. Aug.
Rev.:   Men riding r., carrying small shield
Inscription: Col. Aug. Olb.

>Bibliography:
>Duchalais, *RN*, 1849, p. 98, no. 2 and fig. on p. 97
>Drexler, col. 2724
>Metzger, p. 49, note 6
>Aulock, *J.N.u.G.*, 21, 1971, p. 18, no. 5 & Pl. I

Weight: 6.30 gr. (Paris)
Illustrated example: Paris

Olbasa 2 Plate XXXVIII

Obv.:   Bust of Marcus Aurelius, r., bareheaded
Inscription: Aurel Caesar
Rev.:   Men riding, r., carrying small shield
Inscription: Col. Aug. Olb.

>Bibliography;
>Aulock, *J.N.u.G.* 21, 1971, p. 19, no. 9 & Pl. I

Weight: 5.19 gr. (Leningrad)
Illustrated example: Leningrad
Remarks: Same rev. die as preceding coin.

Olbasa 3 Plate XXXVIII

Obv.:   Bust of Julia Maesa, r.
Inscription: Iulia Maesa M. Aug.
Rev.:   Men riding r., carrying a large shield
Inscription: Col. Iul. Aug. Olbasa

>Bibliography:
>Duchesne, *BCH*, 1877, p. 336
>Löbbecke, *Z. für N.*, 1885, p. 328
>Metzger. p. 49, note 6, Pl. XII f. (rev. only)
>Aulock, *J.N.u.G.*, 1971, p. 21, no. 27 & Pl. III
>Drexler, col. 2724
>*SNG Fitz.*, Pl. 106, no. 5170
>Lane, II, p. 34, Olbasa 1

Weight: 5.60 gr.-9.18 gr. (examples known to Aulock)
Illustrated example: Paris

Olbasa 4   Plate XXXVIII

Obv.:   Bust of Trebonianus Gallus, r., laureate
Inscription: Imp. C. C. Vib. Trcb. Gallum P.F. Aug.
Rev.:   Men riding r. Shield unclear.
Inscription: Col. Iul. Aug. Olbasenorum

> Bibliography:
> Aulock, *J.N.u.G.*, 1971, p. 23, no. 33 & Pl. III

Weight: 19.50 gr. (Hecht Coll.)
Illustrated example: Hecht Coll.

Palaeopolis 1   Plate XXXIX

Obv.:   Bust of Faustina Jr., r.
Inscription: Φαυστεῖνα Σεβαστή (with variations)
Rev.:   Men standing l. with pine-cone (?)
Inscription: Παλαιοπολειτῶν

> Bibliography:
> Imhoof, *Kl. M.*, II, p. 386, Palaiopolis 1
> Dieudonne, *RN*, 1902, p. 351, no. 99 and Pl. X, 16 (rev. only)
> Grose, III, p. 276, no. 8992, and Pl. 322.16
> Lane, II, p. 34, Palaiopolis 1

Weight: 4.53 gr. (Paris) - 4.91 gr. (Cambridge)
Illustrated example: Cambridge

Palaeopolis 2   Plate XXXIX

Obv.:   Bust of Caracalla, r., bareheaded
Inscription: Αὐ. Κα. Μ. Αὐρ. Ἀντωνεῖνος
Rev.:   Men standing l. with pine-cone (?)
Inscription: Παλεοπολειτῶν

> Bibliography:
> Drexler, col. 2725
> *BMC Lycia*, p. 231, no. 2
> Weber, III, 2, p. 597, no. 7404 and Pl. 266
> Lane, II, p. 34, Palaeopolis 2

Weight: 3.52 gr. (Gotha) - 4.47 gr. (Weber)
Illustrated example: Weber

Palaeopolis 3   Plate XXXIX

Obv.: Bust of Severus Alexander, r., laureate
Inscription: Αὐ. Κ. Μ. Αὐ. Σε. Ἀλέξανδρος
Rev.: Men standing slightly l. with pine-cone and bucranium
Inscription: Παλεοπολειτῶν

> Bibliography:
> Drexler, col. 2724 (this or next coin)
> Svoronos, *JIAN*, 1903, p. 233, no. 528 and Pl. XV, 15 (rev. only)
> Lane, II, p. 34, Palaeopolis 3 and Pl. IX, 10

Weight: 9.48 gr. (Athens)
Illustrated example: Athens

Palaeopolis 4   Plate XXXIX

Obv.: Bust of Severus Alexander, r., laureate
Inscription: Αὐ. Κ. Μ. Αὐ. Σε. Ἀλέξανδρος
Rev.: Men standing r. with pine-cone and bucranium
Inscription: Παλεοπολειτῶν

> Bibliography:
> Imhoof, *Kl. M.*, II, p. 386, Palaeopolis 3

Weight: 7.92 gr. (New York)
Illustrated example: New York

Pappa-Tiberia 1   Plate XXXIX

Obv.: Bust of Antoninus Pius, r., laureate
Inscription: Αὐ. Και. Ἀδρ. Ἀντωνῖνος
Rev.: Men standing r. with pine-cone and bucranium
Inscription: Τιβεριέων Παππηνῶν

> Bibliography:
> Birch, *NC*, 1844, p. 10, no. 1
> Waddington, *RN*, 1853, p. 43
> Drexler, col. 2724
> *BMC Lycia*, p. 233, nos. 1-2 and Pl. XXXVII, 3 (rev. only)

Inv. Wadd., RN, p. 56, no. 3778
SNG Aulock, Pl. 169, nos. 5132-33
SNG Fitz., Pl. 106, no. 5171
Lane, II, p. 34, Pappa-Tiberia 1

Weight: 4.40 gr. (Aulock) - 7.38 gr. (Berlin)
Illustrated example: Istanbul

Parlais 1   Plate XXXIX

Obv.:   Bust of Lucius Verus, r., laureate
Inscription: L. Aurelio Vero
Rev.:   Men standing r. with Antiochene attributes
Inscription: Parlais Co.

   Bibliography:
   Waddington, *RN*, 1883, p. 59, no. 2
   Drexler, col. 2726
   Lane, II, p. 35, Parlais 1 and Pl. X, 2

Weight: 4.19 gr. (Vienna)
Illustrated example: Vienna

Parlais 2   Plate XXXIX

Obv.:   Bust of Lucius Verus, r., laureate
Inscription: L. Aurelius Verus
Rev.:   Men standing r. with pine-cone and rooster (?)
Inscription: Iul. Aug. Col. Parla

   Bibliography:
   Drexler, col. 2726
   SNG Aulock, Pl. 169, no. 5135
   Lane, II, p. 35, Parlais 2

Weight: 5.97 gr. (Aulock)
Illustrated example: Aulock

Parlais 3   Plate XXXIX

Obv.:   Bust of Marcus Aurelius, r., laureate
Inscription: M. Aur. Antoninus
Rev.:   Men standing r. with pine-cone and rooster (?)
Inscription: Iul. Aug. Ha. Col. Parla.

Bibliography:
Lane, II, p. 35, Parlais 3 and Pl. X, 3

Weight: 5.94 gr. (New York)
Illustrated example: New York

Parlais 4   Plate XXXIX

Obv.: Bust of Commodus, r., laureate (young, bearded)
Inscription: Imp. C. Aur. Commo. Aug. (with variations)
Rev.: Men standing r. with pine-cone and rooster (?)
Inscription: Iul. Aug. Ha. Col. Parla (with variations)

Bibliography:
Waddington, *RN*, 1883, p. 59, no. 3
Drexler, col. 2726
Inv. Wadd., *RN*, 1898, no. 4792
Imhoof-Blumer, *SNR*, 1908, p. 88, Parlais 3
Hill, *NC*, 1914, p. 311, no. 35
SNG Aulock, Pl. 300, no. 8615
Lane, II, p. 35, Parlais 4 and Pl. X, 4

Weight: 4.86 gr. (Gotha) - 5.91 gr. (Aulock)
Illustrated example: Aulock

Parlais 5   Plate XXXIX

Obv.: Bust of Septimius Severus, l., laureate
Inscription: Imp. Caes. L. Sep. Severus (with variations)
Rev.: Men standing r. with pine-cone and bucranium
Inscription: Iul. Aug. Col. Parlais

Bibliography:
Waddington, *RN*, 1883, p. 59, no. 5
Imhoof, p. 347, no. 118
Drexler, col. 2726
Inv. Wadd., *RN*, 1898, p. 201, no. 4793
SNG Cop., *Lycaonia*, Pl. I, no. 13
SNG Aulock, Pl. 300, no. 8617
SNG Fitz., Pl. 107, no. 5218
Lane, II, p. 35, Parlais 5; III, p. 105, no. 17

Weight: 3.54 gr. (Athens) - 5.78 gr. (Copenhagen)
Illustrated example: Istanbul

Parlais 6   Plate XL

Obv.:   Bust of Septimius Severus, r., laureate
Inscription: Imp. Caes. L. Sep. Severus P.
Rev.:   Men standing r. with pine-cone and bucranium
Inscription: Iul. Aug. Col. Parla

> Bibliography:
> SNG *Aulock*, Pl. 169, no. 5136: Pl. 300, no. 8616
> Lane, II, p. 35, Parlais 6

Weight: 5.50 gr.-5.88 gr. (Aulock)
Illustrated example: Aulock

Parlais 7   Plate XL

Obv.:   Bust of Julia Domna, l.
Inscription: Iulia Domna Aug.
Rev.:   Men standing r. with pine-cone and bucranium
Inscription: Iul. Aug. Col. Parlais

> Bibliography:
> Fiorelli, no. 8481
> Waddington, *RN*, 1883, p. 60, no. 8
> Drexler, col. 2726
> *BMC Lycaonia*, p. 11, nos. 1-2, and Pl. II, 5
> *Inv. Wadd.*, *RN*, 1898, p. 201, no. 4794
> Grose, III, p. 284, no. 9041 and Pl. 325.5
> *SNG Cop.*, *Lycaonia*, Pl. I, no. 14
> Lane, II, p. 35, Parlais 7

Weight: 4.35 gr. (Cambridge) - 6.05 gr. (Berlin)
Illustrated example: Athens

Parlais 8   Plate XL

Obv.:   Bust of Julia Domna, r.
Inscription: Iulia Domna
Rev.:   Men standing r. with pine-cone and bucranium
Inscription: Iul. Aug. Col. Parlais

> Bibliography:
> *BMC Lycaonia*, p. 11, no. 3
> *SNG Aulock*, Pl. 169, no. 5137
> Lane, II, p. 35, Parlais 8

Weight: 4.35 gr. (Berlin) - 5.59 gr. (Aulock)
Illustrated example: Aulock

Parlais 9   Plate XL

Obv.:   Bust of Caracalla, r., bareheaded
Inscription: Antonin
Rev.:   Men standing r. with pine-cone and bucranium
Inscription: Iul. Aug. Col. Parlais

> Bibliography:
> Lane, II, p. 35, Parlais 9 and Pl. X, 5

Weight: 5. 36 gr. (New York)
Illustrated example: New York

Prostanna 1   Plate XL

Obv.:   Bust of Septimius Severus, r., laureate
Inscription: Αὐ. Κ. Λ. Σε. Σεουῆρος Π.
Rev.: Men standing, holding scroll and pine-cone in a distyle temple, two lions at his feet, a rooster on either side of his head
Inscription: Προσταννέων

> Bibliography:
> Borrell, *NC*, 1847, p. 96, no. 1
> Roscher, Pl. Ib, no. 14
> Drexler, col. 2724
> Imhoof, *Kl. M.*, II, p. 390, no. 7
> Lane, II, p. 35, Prostanna 1

Weight: 24.87 gr. (Munich)
Illustrated example: Munich

Prostanna 2   Plate XL

Obv.:   Bust of Valerian, r., laureate
Inscription: Αὐ, Και. Πο. Λι. Οὐαλεριανός
Rev.: Men standing l. in distyle temple, holding a pine-cone (?). At his feet, lions; on either side of his head, roosters (?) on shelves. Eagle in pediment. Decoration of four superposed shields (?) on each anta.

Inscription: Προστανντέων

> Bibliography:
> Krzyzanowska, MC, p. 102

Weight: 12.47 gr. (London)
Illustrated example: London

Sagalassus 1   Plate XL

Obv.: Bust of Athena (or Roma?) r. with Corinthian helmet
No inscription
Rev.: Bust of Men, r., cap laureate
Inscription: Σαγαλασ. (with variations)

> Bibliography:
> Drexler, col. 2724
> Imhoof, Kl. M., II, p. 392, Sagalassus 5 and Pl. XIV, no. 10
> Svoronos, JIAN, 1904, p. 388, no. 272 and Pl. XVIII, 10
> Weber, III, ii, p. 598, no. 7408, and Pl. 266
> Grose, III, p. 277, no. 8996, and Pl. 322.19
> SNG Cop., Pisidia, Pl. 7, no. 196-7
> SNG Aulock, Pl. 170, no. 5162

Weight: 2.19 gr. (Copenhagen) - 3.30 gr. (Imhoof)
Illustrated example: Aulock

Sagalassus 2   Plate XL

Obv.: Bust of Hermes, r.
No inscription
Rev.: Bust of Men, r. No laurel wreath.
Inscription: Σαγα.

> Bibliography:
> Drexler, col. 2724
> Imhoof, Kl. M., II, p. 392, Sagalassus 4 and Pl. XIV, 9
> Lane, II, p. 36, Sagalassus 2

Weight: 3.30 gr. (Berlin)
Illustrated example: Berlin

Sagalassus 3   Plate XLI

Obv.: Bust of Herakles, r.
No inscription
Rev.: Bust of Men, r.
Inscription: Σαγαλα.

> Bibliography: none

Weight: 2.48 gr. (Berlin)
Illustrated example: Berlin

Sagalassus 4   Plate XLI

Obv.: Bust of Hadrian, r., laureate
Inscription: Ἀδριανὸς Καῖσαρ Ὀλύμπιος
Rev.: Men standing l. with pine-cone, a bull standing at his feet
Inscription: Σαγαλασσέων

> Bibliography:
> Borrell, *NC*, 1847, p. 97, no. 2
> Roscher, Pl. Ia, no. 16 (rev. only)
> Drexler, col. 2724
> *BMC Lycia*, p. 242, no. 12
> Grose, III, p. 278, no. 9001 and Pl. 323.4
> Lane, II, p. 36, Sagalassus 3

Weight: 10.56 gr. (Cambridge) - 11.70 gr. (Vienna)
Illustrated example: Cambridge

Sagalassus 5   Plate XLI

Obv.: Bust of Hadrian, r., laureate
Inscription: Ἀδρια. Καισ.
Rev.: Bust of Men, r., cap laureate
Inscription: Σαγαλασ.

> Bibliography:
> Drexler, col. 2724
> Imhoof, *Kl. M.*, II, p. 392, no. 9

Weight: 9.74 gr. (Berlin)
Illustrated example: Berlin

Sagalassus 6 Plate XLI

Obv.: Bust of Marcus Aurelius, r., laureate
Inscription: Αὐτ. Και. 'Αντωνιν.
Rev.: Men riding l.
Inscription: Σαγαλασσέων

> Bibliography:
> *Inv. Wadd.*, *RN*, 1898, p. 59, no. 3842
> Imhoof, *Kl. M.*, II, p. 393, no. 9a
> *SNG Aulock*, Pl. 170, no. 5170
> Lane, II, p. 36, Sagalassus 4

Weight: 9.70 gr. (Aulock) - 9.75 gr. (Paris)
Illustrated example: Aulock

Sagalassus 7 Plate XLI

Obv.: Bust of Septimius Severus, r., laureate
Inscription: 'Α. Και. Λ. Σ. Σεουηρ. Αὐγ.
Rev.: Bust of Men, r.
Inscription: Σαγαλασσέων

> Bibliography:
> Waddington, *RN*, 1853, p. 44, no. 4
> Drexler, col. 2724
> *Inv. Wadd.*, *RN*, 1898, p. 59, no. 3843
> Lane, II, p. 36, Sagalassus 5 and Pl. X, 6

Weight: 1.73 gr. (Gotha) - 2.86 gr. (Paris)
Illustrated example: Paris

Sagalassus 8 Plate XLI

Obv.: Bust of Septimius Severus, r., laureate
Inscription: Αὐτ. Και. Λ. Σεπ. Σεουῆρος Αὐγ. Περτι.
Rev.: Men standing l. with pine-cone and staff
Inscription: Σαγαλασσέων

> Bibliography: none

Weight: 15.02 gr. (Berlin) - 15.55 gr. (Leningrad)
Illustrated example: Leningrad

Sagalassus 9   Plate XLI

Obv.: Bust of Caracalla, r., laureate
Inscription: Αὐ. Κ. Μ. Αὐ. 'Αντωνῖνος
Rev.: Bust of Men, r.
Inscription: Σαγαλασσέων

    Bibliography:
    Grose, III, p. 278, no. 9009 and Pl. 323, 6
    Lane, II, p. 36, Sagalassus 6

Weight: 3.65 (Cambridge)
Illustrated example: Cambridge

Sagalassus 10   Plate XLI

Obv.: Bust of Caracalla, r., laureate, beardless
Inscription: Αὐτ. Κ. Μ. Αὐρ. 'Αντωνῖνος
Rev.: Men riding l.
Inscription:

    Bibliography:
    F. Baillion, *RBN*, 1933, pp. 149-151

Weight: 8.65 gr. (Brussels)
Illustrated example: Brussels

Sagalassus 11   Plate XLI

Obv.: Bust of Geta, l.
Inscription: Γέτας Καισ.
Rev.: Bust of Men, r.
Inscription: Σαγαλασσέων

    Bibliography:
    Imhoof-Blumer, *SNR*, 1908, p. 81, no. 3

Weight: 1.50 gr. (Berlin)
Illustrated example: Berlin

Sagalassus 12   Plate XLI

Obv.: Bust of Macrinus, r., laureate
Inscription: 'Ιο. Με. Λε. Σευηρ. Μακρεῖνος Αὐ.
Rev.: Men standing l. with staff and patera. Indistinct object at feet.
Inscription: Σαγαλασσέων

> Bibliography:
> Drexler, col. 2724
> Lane, II, p. 36, Sagalassus 7 and Pl. X, 7; p. 37, Sagalassus 17 and Pl. XI, 1

Weight: 7.34 gr. (Oxford) - 8.61 gr. (Vienna)
Illustrated example: Vienna

Sagalassus 13   Plate XLII

Obv.: Bust of Severus Alexander, r., laureate
Inscription: 'Α. Κ. 'Αλέξανδρος
Rev.: Men standing l. with patera and staff
Inscription: Σαγαλασ.

> Bibliography:
> Imhoof-Blumer, *SNR*, 1908, p. 81, Sagalassus 4

Weight: 1.13 gr. (Berlin)
Illustrated example: Berlin

Sagalassus 14   Plate XLII

Obv.: Bust of Julia Mamaea, r.
Inscription: 'Ιουλία Μαμέα Σεβ.
Rev.: Men standing l. with patera and staff
Inscription: Σαγαλασσέων

> Bibliography:
> *SNG Aulock*, Pl. 171, no. 5183
> Lane, II, p. 36, Sagalassus 8

Weight: 12.46 gr. (Aulock)
Illustrated example: Aulock

Sagalassus 15 Plate XLII

Obv.: Bust of Maximinus, r., laureate
Inscription: Αὐ. Κ. Γ. 'Ιου. Μαξιμι. Αὐγ. (with variations)
Rev.: Men standing l. with patera and staff
Inscription: Σαγαλασσέων

    Bibliography:
    Imhoof, *Kl. M.*, II, p. 394, no. 14
    Svoronos, *JIAN*, 1903, p. 236, no. 548
    Lane, II, p. 36, Sagalassus 9 and Pl. X, no. 8
    Kraft, Pl. 108, no. 15

Weight: 8.67 gr. (Istanbul) - 10.90 gr. (Athens)
Illustrated example: Istanbul

Sagalassus 16 Plate XLII

Obv.: Bust of Maximus, r.
Inscription: Μαξιμο.
Rev.: Men standing l. with patera and staff, no cloak
Inscription: Σαγαλασ.

    Bibliography:
    Imhoof, *Kl. M.*, II, p. 394, no. 15

Weight: 1.36 gr. (Berlin)
Illustrated example: Berlin

Sagalassus 17 Plate XLII

Obv.: Bust of Gordian III, r.
Inscription: Αὐτ. Κ. Μ. 'Αν. Γορδιανός
Rev.: Men standing l. with patera and staff
Inscription: Σαγαλασσέων

    Bibliography:
    Inv. Wadd., *RN*, 1898, p. 60, no. 3864
    Lane, II, p. 36, no. 10 and Pl. X, no. 9

Weight: 8.31 gr. (Paris)
Illustrated example: Paris

Sagalassus 18 Plate XLII

Obv.: Bust of Otacilia Severa, r.
Inscription: Μαρ. 'Ωτ. Σεουῆραν Σ.
Rev.: Men standing l. with patera and staff
Inscription: Σαγαλασσέων

> Bibliography:
> Drexler, col. 2724
> *SNG Aulock*, Pl. 171, no. 5187
> Lane, II, p. 36, Sagalassus 11

Weight: 12.30 gr. (Aulock)
Illustrated example: Aulock

Sagalassus 19 Plate XLII

Obv.: Bust of Trajan Decius, r., laureate
Inscription: Αὐ. Κ. Γ. Μ. Τρ. Δέκιος
Rev.: Bust of Men with starry cap, laureate, r.
Inscription: Σαγαλασσέων of which the initial sigma is made to resemble a crescent moon.

> Bibliography:
> Imhoof, *Kl. M.*, II, p. 395, no. 19 and Pl. XIV, 13 (rev. only)
> *SNG Cop.*, *Pisidia*, Pl. 8, no. 210
> Lane, II, p. 36, Sagalassus 12

Weight: 11.66 gr. (Copenhagen) - 12.14 gr. (Vienna)
Illustrated example: Copenhagen

Sagalassus 20 Plate XLII

Obv.: Bust of Herennia Etruscilla, r.
Inscription: faint
Rev.: Bust of Men, r.
Inscription: Σαγαλασσέων of which the initial sigma again resembles a crescent moon.

> Bibliography:
> *Inv. Wadd.*, *RN*, 1898, p. 61, no. 3870

Weight: 12.68 gr. (Paris)
Illustrated example: Paris

Sagalassus 21   Plate XLII

Obv.: Bust of Trebonianus Gallus, r., laureate
Inscription: Αὐ. Κα. Γα. Οὐι. Τρ. Γάλλος
Rev.: Men standing l. with patera and staff
Inscription: Σαγαλασσέων

> Bibliography:
> Lane, II, p. 36, Sagalassus 13
> *SNG Cop.*, *Pisidia*, Pl. 8, no. 211
> Lane, II, p. 36, Sagalassus 13

Weight: 10.00 gr. (Copenhagen)
Illustrated example: Copenhagen

Sagalassus 22   Plate XLII

Obv.: Bust of Gallienus, r., laureate
Inscription: ’Α. Κ. Π. Λη. Γαλλιηνός
Rev.: Men standing l. with patera and staff
Inscription: Σαγαλασσέων

> Bibliography:
> Grose, III, p. 279, no. 9006 and Pl. 323.9
> Lane, II, p. 36, Sagalassus 14

Weight: 10.48 gr. (Cambridge)
Illustrated example: Cambridge

Sagalassus 23   Plate XLIII

Obv.: Bust of Gallienus, radiate, r.
Inscription: ’Α. Κ. Π. Λο. Γαλιηνόνς
Rev.: Bust of Men, r.
Inscription: Σαγαλασσέων

> Bibliography:
> Weber, III, ii, p. 599 no. 7414 and Pl. 266
> Lane, II, p. 36, Sagalassus 15

Weight: 8.46 gr. (London)
Illustrated example: London

Sagalassus 24   Plate XLIII

Obv.: Bust of Salonina, r.
Inscription: Σε. Σαλωνεῖνα
Rev.: Men standing l. with patera and staff
Inscription: Σαγαλασσέων

    Bibliography: none

Weight: 13.54 gr. (Baldwin's)
Illustrated example: Baldwin's

Sagalassus 25   Plate XLIII

Obv.: Bust of Claudius Gothicus, r., laureate
Inscription: Αὐ. Κ. Μ. Αὐρ. Κλαύδιον Σεβ. I
Rev.: Men standing l. with patera and staff
Inscription: Σαγαλασσέων

    Bibliography:
    BMC Lycia, p. 249, no. 47
    Inv. Wadd., *RN*, 1898, p. 62, no. 3886
    A. Markl, *NZ*, 1900, p. 172, no. 48 and Pl. XI, 48
    SNG Aulock, Pl. 300, no. 8631
    Lane, II, p. 36, Sagalassus 16 and Pl. X, 10

Weight: 15.52 gr. (Vienna) - 18.72 gr. (Aulock)
Illustrated example: London

Sagalassus 26   Plate XLIII

Obv.: Bust of Claudius Gothicus, r., laureate
Inscription: Αὐ. Κ. Μ. Αὐρ. Κλαύδιον I
Rev.: Men riding l. on horse which ambles slowly
Inscription: Σαγαλασσέων

    Bibliography:
    Roscher, Pl. Ib, no. 12
    Drexler, col. 2724
    BMC Lycia, p. 249, no. 46
    A. Markl, *NZ*, 1900, p. 173, no. 49 and Pl. XI, 49
    SNG Cop., *Pisidia*, Pl. 8, no. 221
    Lane, II, p. 37, Sagalassus 18

Weight: 13.40 gr. (Copenhagen) - 20.89 gr. (Vienna)
Illustrated example: Copenhagen

Sagalassus 27 Plate XLIII

Alliance coin of Sagalassus and Side
Obv.: Bust of Volusian, r., laureate
Inscription: 'Α. Κ. Γάλλος Οὐολουσσιανο.
Rev.: Men standing with staff on l. of coin, Athena on r., clasping hands
Inscription: Σαγαλασσέων α' Πισι. Σιδηδῶν ὁμόνοια

    Bibliography: none

Weight: 17.70 gr. (New York)
Illustrated example: New York
Remarks: This would seem to be the same as the alleged coin of Side, from the time of Gordian III, referred to by Drexler, col. 2720, on the basis of Mionnet and other older publications.

Seleuceia 1 Plate XLIV

Obv.: Bust of Hadrian, r., laureate
Inscription: Καῖσαρ 'Αδριανός
Rev.: Men standing r. with staff and bucranium, left hand on hip
Inscription: Κλαυδιοσελευκέων

    Bibliography:
    Drexler, col. 2725
    Lane, II, p. 37, Seleuceia 1 and Pl. XI, 2

Weight: 5.08 gr. (Paris) - 6.41 gr. (London)
Illustrated example: London
Remarks: This is the standard type at Seleuceia, and probably derives from a local cult statue, as it does not occur elsewhere.

Seleuceia 2 Plate XLIV

Obv.: Bust of Septimius Severus, r., laureate
Inscription illegible
Rev.: Men standing r. with staff and bucranium, hand on hip
Inscription illegible

    Bibliography: none

Weight: 18.75 gr. (Vienna)
Illustrated example: Vienna
Remarks: The Vienna example bears the notation, "Erutus ad Mauerstein in gurgite Danuvii."

Seleuceia 3   Plate XLIV

Obv.: Bust of Caracalla, r., laureate
Inscription: Αὐ. Καισ. Μ. Αὐρ. 'Αντωνεῖνος
Rev.: Men standing r. with staff and bucranium, hand on hip
Inscription: Κλαυδιοσελευκέων

> Bibliography:
> Drexler, col. 2725
> *SNG Aulock*, Pl. 173, no. 5226
> Lane, II, p. 37, Seleuceia 2

Weight: 7.98 gr. (Gotha) - 8.86 gr. (Aulock)
Illustrated examples: Aulock

Seleuceia 4   Plate XLIV

Obv.: Bust of Caracalla, r., laureate
Inscription: Αὐτ. Καισ. Μ. Αὐρ. 'Αντωνεῖνος
Rev.: Men standing r. with staff and bucranium, hand on hip
Inscription: Κλαυδιοσελευκέων

> Bibliography: none

Weight: 20.83 gr. (Berlin)
Illustrated example: Berlin
Remarks: Similar to preceding, except much larger denomination.

Seleuceia 5   Plate XLIV

Obv.: Bust of Julia Paula, r.
Inscription: 'Ιου. Κορ. Παῦλα Σε.
Rev.: Men riding r.
Inscription: Κλαυδιοσελευκέων

> Bibliography:
> Imhoof-Blumer, *SNR*, 1908, p. 83, Seleuceia 1

Weight: 5.22 gr. (Vienna) - 6.67 gr. (Munich)
Illustrated example: Vienna

Seleuceia 6   Plate XLIV

Obv.: Bust of Severus Alexander, r., laureate
Inscription: Αὐτ. Κ. Μ. Αὐ. ᾿Αλέξανδρος
Rev.: Men standing r., with bucranium and staff, hand on hip
Inscription: Κλαυδιοσελευκέων

> Bibliography:
> Roscher, Pl. Ia, 13 (rev. only)
> Drexler, col. 2725
> *Inv. Wadd.*, *RN*, 1898, p. 63, no. 3901
> *SNG Aulock*, Pl. 173, no. 5231
> Lane, II, p. 37, Seleucia 3

Weight: 7.09 gr. (Paris) - 10.24 gr. (Aulock)
Illustrated example: Aulock

Seleuceia 7   Plate XLIV

Obv.: Bust of Severus Alexander, r., laureate
Inscription: Αὐτ. Κ. Μ. Αὐ. Σευ. ᾿Αλέξανδρος
Rev.: Men riding r.
Inscription: Κλαυδιοσελευκέων

> Bibliography:
> Roscher, Pl. Ib, no. 11 (rev. only)
> Drexler, col. 2725
> Imhoof, *Kl. M.*, II, p. 399, Seleuceia 5
> *SNG Cop.*, *Pisidia*, Pl. 9, no. 227
> Lane, II, p. 37, Seleuceia 7

Weight: 7.11 gr. (Copenhagen) - 8.59 gr. (Leningrad)
Illustrated example: Leningrad

Seleuceia 8   Plate XLIV

Obv.: Bust of Julia Mamaea, r.
Inscription: ᾿Ιουλίαν Μαμέαν Σε.
Rev.: Men standing r. with staff and bucranium, hand on hip
Inscription: Κλαυδιοσελευκέων

Bibliography:
Inv. Wadd., RN, 1898, p. 63, no. 3903 and Pl. IV, 8 (rev. only)
Weber, III, ii, p. 600, no. 7416 and Pl. 267
SNG Aulock, Pl. 173, no. 5233
Lane, II, p. 37, Seleuceia 4
Kraft, Pl. 108, no. 12

Weight: 6.74 gr. (Weber) - 8.10 gr. (Leningrad)
Illustrated example: Leningrad

Seleuceia 9   Plate XLIV

Obv.: Bust of Maximinus, r., laureate
Inscription: Αὐ. Κ. Γ. 'Ιου. Μαξιμι 'Α.
Rev.: Men standing r. with staff and bucranium, l. hand on hip
Inscription: Κλαυδιοσελευκέων

Bibliography:
Inv. Wadd., RN, 1898, p. 63, no. 3905
SNG Aulock, Pl. 173, no. 5235
Lane, II, p. 37, Seleuceia 5

Weight: 8.46 gr. (Aulock) - 9.14 gr. (Paris)
Illustrated example: Aulock

Seleuceia 10   Plate XLIV

Obv.: Bust of Maximus, r., bareheaded
Inscription: Γ. 'Ιου. Μάξιμος
Rev.: Men standing with staff and bucranium, hand on hip
Inscription: Κλαυδιοσελευκέων

Bibliography:
Inv. Wadd., RN, 1898, p. 63, no. 3906

Weight: 9.45 gr. (Paris)
Illustrated example: Paris

Seleuceia 11   Plate XLV

Obv.: Bust of Gordian III, r., laureate
Inscription: Αὐ. Κ. Μαρ. 'Αν. Γορδιανός Εὐ. Σε.
Rev.: Men standing r., with staff and bucranium, hand on hip
Inscription: Κλαυδιοσελευκέων

Bibliography:
Imhoof, *Kl. M.*, II, p. 399, Seleuceia 7

Weight: 8.88 gr. (Munich) - 10.13 gr. (Leningrad)
Illustrated example: Munich

Seleuceia 12   Plate XLV

Obv.: Bust of Gordian III, r., laureate
Inscription: Αὐ. Κ. Μαρ. 'Αν. Γορδιανὸς Εὐ. Σε.
Rev.: Men riding r.
Inscription: Κλαυδιοσελευκέων

> Bibliography:
> Drexler, col. 2725
> *SNG Cop., Pisidia*, Pl. 9, no. 230
> Lane, II, p. 37, Seleuceia 8

Weight: 7—89 gr. (Paris) - 9.92 gr. (London)
Illustrated example: Leningrad

Seleuceia 13   Plate XLV

Obv.: Bust of Tranquillina, r.
Inscription: .... Τρανκυλλῖνα Σε.
Rev.: Men riding r.
Inscription: Κλαυδιοσελευκέων

> Bibliography: none

Weight: 9.57 gr. (Vienna)
Illustrated example: Vienna

Seleuceia 14   Plate XLV

Obv.: Bust of Claudius Gothicus, r., laureate
Inscription: Αὐ. Κ. Μ. Αὐρ. Κλαύδιος
Rev.: Men standing r. with staff and bucranium, hand on hip
Inscription: Κλαυδιοσελευκέων

> Bibliography:
> Drexler, col. 2725
> A. Markl, *NZ*, 1900, p. 181-2, nos. 79-80, and Pl. XIV, 80

SNG Aulock, Pl. 300, no. 8633
Lane, II, p. 37, Seleuceia 6 and Pl. XI, 3

Weight: 14.81 gr. (Vienna) - 20.40 gr. (Imhoof)
Illustrated example: Leningrad

Sibidunda 1   Plate XLV

Obv.: Bust of Elagabalus (?) r., laureate
Inscription: Αὐ. Κ. Μ. Αὐ. 'Αντωνεῖνος
Rev.: Men standing l. with pine-cone and staff, foot on bucranium
Inscription: Σιβιδουνδέων

> Bibliography:
> Drexler, col. 2718
> BMC Phrygia, p. 378, no. 7, and Pl. XLIV, 2
> Lane, II, p. 37, Sibidunda 1

Weight: 4.29 gr. (Paris) - 5.32 gr. (London)
Illustrated example: Paris

Timbrias 1   Plate XLV

Obv.: Bust of Men, r.
Inscription: A B P (?)
Rev.: Caps of the Dioscuri, with stars
Inscription: Τιμβριαδέων

> Bibliography:
> Imhoof, *Kl. M.*, II, p. 413, Timbrias 1
> Lane, II, p. 38, Timbrias 1 and Pl. XI, no. 4

Weight: 2.85 gr.-3.08 gr. (Berlin)
Illustrated example: Berlin

Timbrias 2   Plate XLV

Obv.: Bust of Julia Domna, r.
Inscription: 'Ιουλία Δο. Σεβαστή
Rev.: Men standing l. with patera (?) and staff. Altar (?) at feet.
Inscription: Τιμβριαδέων

> Bibliography: none

Weight: 12.65 gr. (Lewis Coll.)
Illustrated example: Lewis Coll.

Timbrias 3   Plate XLV

Obv.: Bust of Caracalla, r., laureate
Inscription: Αὐ. Κ. Μ. ’Αντωειν.
Rev.: Men standing l. with staff and patera, altar (?) at feet
Inscription: Τιμβριαδέων

> Bibliography:
> Lane, II, p. 38, Timbrias 2 and Pl. XI, 5

Weight: 7.06 gr. (Leningrad) - 7.91 gr. (Berlin)
Illustrated example: Leningrad

Timbrias 4   Plate XLV

Obv.: Bust of Elagabalus, r., laureate
Inscription: Αὐ. Κ. Μ. Αὐ. ’Αντωνεῖνος
Rev.: Men standing l. with patera and staff, bull at feet
Inscription: Τιμβριαδέων

> Bibliography:
> *Inv. Wadd.*, *RN*, 1898, p. 70, nos. 4028-9 and Pl. IV, 8 (rev. only)
> Svoronos, *JIAN*, 1903, p. 250, no. 700 and Pl. 16, 16

Weight: 9.28 gr. (Athens) - 10.57 gr. (Munich)
Illustrated example: Athens

Attaleia 1   Plate XLV

Obv.: Bust of Caracalla, r., laureate
Inscription: Αὐτ. Μ. Αὐ. ’Αντωνεῖνος
Rev.: Men standing l. with pine-cone and staff, foot on bucranium
Inscription: ’Ατταλέων

> Bibliography:
> Imhoof, *Kl. M.*, II, p. 323, Attaleia 5

Weight: 7.78 gr.-10.88 gr. (Berlin)
Illustrated example: Berlin

Attaleia 2   Plate XLVI

Obv.: Bust of Geta, l., laureate
Inscription: ’Α. Σ. Γέτας Καῖσαρ

Rev.: Bust of Men, r.
Inscription: Ἀτταλέων

> Bibliography:
> Svoronos, *JIAN*, 1903, p. 201, no. 227

Weight: 5.17 gr. (Athens)
Illustrated example: Athens

Sillyon 1   Plate XLVI

Obv.: Bust of Antoninus Pius, r., laureate
Inscription: Αὐτοκρα. Καῖσαρ
Rev.: Men riding r.
Inscription: Σιλλυέων

> Bibliography:
> *Inv. Wadd.*, *RN*, 1898, p. 41, no. 3523
> Lane, II, p. 38, Sillyon 1 and Pl. XI, 7

Weight: 7.45 gr. (Istanbul) - 9.16 gr. (Paris)
Illustrated example: Istanbul

Sillyon 2   Plate XLVI

Obv.: Bust of Faustina, Jr., r.
Inscription: Φαυστῖνα Σεβαστή
Rev.: Men riding r.
Inscription: Σιλλυέων

> Bibliography:
> Drexler, col. 2720
> *SNG Aulock*, Pl. 159, no. 4871
> Lane, II, p. 38, Sillyon 2

Weight: 23.86 gr. (Aulock) - 25.09 gr. (Leningrad)
Illustrated example: Aulock

Sillyon 3   Plate XLVI

Obv.: Bust of Lucilla, r.
Inscription: Λουκίλλα Σεβαστή
Rev.: Men standing r. with staff, pine-cone, and bucranium
Inscription: Σιλλυέων

Bibliography: none
Weight: unavailable
Illustrated example: Hecht collection

Sillyon 4   Plate XLVI

Obv.: Bust of Lucilla, r.
Inscription: Λουκίλλα Σεβαστή
Rev.: Bust of Men, r., stars on cap
Inscription: Σιλλυέων

  Bibliography:
  SNG Aulock, Pl. 159, no. 4872
  Lane, II, p. 38, Sillyon 3

Weight: 9.55 gr. (Aulock) - 10.32 gr. (Istanbul)
Illustrated example: Istanbul

Sillyon 5   Plate XLVI

Obv.: Bust of Commodus, as Caesar, r., laureate
Inscription: Αὐτ. Καῖσαρ Λ. Αὐρη. Κόμοδος
Rev.: Men riding r.
Inscription: Σιλλυέων

  Bibliography:
  SNG Aulock, Pl. 159, no. 4873
  Lane, II, p. 38, Sillyon 4

Weight: 25.45 gr. (Aulock)
Illustrated example: Aulock

Sillyon 6   Plate XLVI

Obv.: Bust of Commodus, as Augustus, r., laureate
Inscription: Μαρ. Αὐ. Κομμ. ’Αντωνεῖνος
Rev.: Men riding l.
Inscription: Σιλλυέων

  Bibliography:
  SNG Aulock, Pl. 159, no. 4874
  Lane, II, p. 38, Sillyon 5
  Vermeule, *Roman Imperial Art in Greece and Asia Minor*, 1968, p. 167-8, fig. 103

Weight: 27.89 gr. (Aulock)
Illustrated example: Aulock

Sillyon 7   Plate XLVII

Obv.: Bust of Commodus, r., laureate
Inscription: Λ. Αὐρηλ. Κόμοδος
Rev.: Men standing l. with pine-cone and staff
Inscription: Σιλλυέων

    Bibliography:
    Inv. Wadd., *RN*, 1898, p. 41, no. 3525
    Lane, II, p. 38, Sillyon 6 and Pl. XI, 8

Weight: 23.99 gr.-29.57 gr. (Paris)
Illustrated example: Paris

Sillyon 8   Plate XLVII

Obv.: Bust of Commodus, beardless, r., laureate
Inscription: Αὐτ. Καῖσαρ Λ. Αὐρηλ. Κόμοδος
Rev.: Bust of Men., r., no stars on cap
Inscription: Σιλλυέων

    Bibliography:
    Münzen und Medaillen, Cat. 41, p. 65, no. 507 and Pl. 30

Weight: 30.83 gr. (Münzen und Medaillen)
Illustrated example: Münzen und Medaillen

Sillyon 9   Plate XLVII

Obv.: Bust of Commodus, r., bearded, laureate, with aegis
Inscription: Μαρ. Αὐ. Κομμ. Ἀντωνεῖνος
Rev.: Men riding r.
Inscription: Σιλλυέων

    Bibliography:
    Münzen und Medaillen 41, p. 65, no. 508 and Pl. 30

Weight: 25.10 gr. (Winterthur) - 25.68 gr. (Münzen und Medaillen)
Illustrated example: Münzen und Medaillen

Sillyon 10   Plate XLVII

Obv.: Bust of Septimius Severus, r., laureate
Inscription: Αὐ. Και. Λ. Σεπ. Σεουῆρος Πε.
Rev.: Men standing r. with pine-cone and staff, foot on bucranium
Inscription: Σιλλυέων

> Bibliography:
> *BMC Lycia*, p. 166, no. 4 and Pl. XXIX, 8 (rev. only)
> Lane, II, p. 38, Sillyon 7

Weight: 23.39 gr. (London)
Illustrated example: London

Sillyon 11   Plate XLVIII

Obv.: Bust of Septimius Severus, r., laureate
Inscription: Αὐ. Κ. Λ. Σ. Σεουῆρος Περ.
Rev.: Men standing l. with staff and pine-cone, foot on bucranium
Inscription: Σιλλυέων

> Bibliography:
> Drexler, col. 2720 (these coins in general)
> *BMC Lycia*, p. 166, no. 6
> Svoronos, *JIAN*, 1903, p. 219, no. 418
> *SNG Cop.*, Lycia, Pl. 13, no. 445
> *SNG Aulock*, Pl. 159, no. 4879
> Lane, II, p. 38, Sillyon 8 and 10

Weight: 4.11 gr. (Copenhagen) - 4.96 gr. (London)
Illustrated example: Athens
Remarks: Much smaller denomination than the preceding.

Sillyon 12   Plate XLVIII

Obv.: Head of Septimius Severus, r., laureate
Inscription: Αὐ. Κ. Λ. Σεουῆρον Περ.
Rev.: Men standing r. with staff and pine-cone, foot on bucranium
Inscription: Σιλλυέων

> Bibliography:
> *BMC Lycia*, p. 166, no. 5
> Svoronos, *JIAN*, 1903, p. 219, no. 419

Weight: 3.98 gr. (London) - 5.25 gr. (Munich)
Illustrated example: New York
Remarks: Also small denomination.

Sillyon 13   Plate XLVIII

Obv.: Bust of Septimius Severus, r., laureate
Inscription: Αὐ. Κ. Λ. Σεουῆρος Πε.
Rev.: Men standing r. with pine-cone and staff, l. foot on bucranium
Inscription: Σιλλυέων

> Bibliography:
> *SNG Aulock*, Pl. 297, no. 8555

Weight: 9.70 gr. (Aulock) - 9.78 gr. (London)
Illustrated example: Aulock
Remarks: This would seem to be intended for an intermediate denomination.

Sillyon 14   Plate XLVIII

Obv.: Bust of Septimius Severus, r.
Inscription: Αὐτ. Κ. Λ. Σεπτου. Σεουῆρος Πε.
Rev.: Men riding l.
Inscription: Σιλλυέων

> Bibliography:
> Drexler, col. 2720
> *BMC Lycia*, p. 165, no. 3 and Pl. XXIX, 7 (rev. only)
> *SNG Cop.*, Pl. 13, no. 444
> *SNG Aulock*, Pl. 159, no. 4876; Pl. 297, no. 8553
> Lane, II, p. 39, Sillyon 12
> Münzen und Medaillen, Cat. 41, page 65, no. 510 and Pl. 31

Weight: 23.86 gr. (Aulock) - 30.36 gr. (Münzen und Medaillen)
Illustrated example: Aulock

Sillyon 15   Plate XLVIII

Obv.: Bust of Septimius Severus, r., laureate
Inscription: Αὐτ. Κ. Λ. Σεπτου. Σεουῆρος Πε.

Rev.: Men riding r.
Inscription: Σιλλυέων

> Bibliography:
> SNG Aulock, Pl. 297, no. 8554

Weight: 23.16 gr. (Paris) - 27.86 gr. (Vienna)
Illustrated example: Aulock

Sillyon 16 Plate XLVIII

Obv.: Bust of Caracalla, r., laureate
Inscription: Αὐ. Κ. Μ. Αὐ. 'Αν......
Rev.: Men standing r. with pine-cone and staff
Inscription: Σιλλυέων

> Bibliography: none

Weight: 11.84 gr. (Munich) - 12.00 gr. (Evelpides)
Illustrated example: Evelpides

Sillyon 17 Plate XLVIII

Obv.: Bust of Caracalla, r., laureate
Inscription: Μ. Αὐ. 'Αντωνεῖνος
Rev.: Bust of Men., r.
Inscription: Σιλλυέων

> Bibliography: none

Weight: 4.45 gr. (Berlin)
Illustrated example: Berlin

Sillyon 18 Plate XLIX

Obv.: Bust of Geta, r., youthful, bareheaded
Inscription: Αὐ. Κ. Μ. 'Αντωνῖνον
Rev.: Men standing l. with patera and staff. To the left, an altar.
Inscription: Σιλλυέων

> Bibliography:
> Svoronos, *JIAN*, 1903, p. 219, no. 420 and Pl. XIV, 8 (rev. only)
> Lane, II, p. 39, Sillyon 13 and Pl. XI, 10 (rev. only)

Sillyon 19 Plate XLIX

Obv.: Bust of Geta, r., bearded, laureate
Inscription: Αὐ. Κ. Πο. Σε. Γέτας
Rev.: Men riding r.
Inscription: Σιλλυέων

> Bibliography:
> Artemis Antiquities, Cat. 4, 1970, no. 354 (now J. L. Mossop coll.)

Weight: 22.53 gr. (Mossop)
Illustrated example: Mossop

Sillyon 20 Plate XLIX

Obv.: Bust of Geta, r., younger than preceding coin
Inscription: Λ. Σεπ. Γέτας Και.
Rev.: Men riding r.
Inscription: Σιλλυέων

> Bibliography:
> Drexler, col. 2720

Weight: 28.11 gr. (Berlin)
Illustrated example: Berlin

Sillyon 21 Plate XLIX

Obv.: Bust of Geta, r., laureate, unbearded
Inscription: Αὐ. Κ. Πο. Σε. Γέτας
Rev.: Bust of Men, r.
Inscription: Σιλλυέων

> Bibliography:
> Drexler, col. 2720
> Imhoof, *Kl. M.*, II, p. 352, Sillyon 13
> Svoronos, *JIAN*, 1903, p. 219, no. 422

Weight: 4.54 gr. (Athens) - 5.07 gr. (Paris)
Illustrated example: Athens

Sillyon 22 Plate L

Obv.: Bust of Macrinus, r., laureate
Inscription: Αὐτ. Και. Μ. 'Οπελ. Σευ. Μακρ.
Rev.: Men riding l.
Inscription: Σιλλυέων

   Bibliography: none

Weight: 22.80 gr. (Paris)
Illustrated example: Paris

Sillyon 23 Plate L

Obv.: Bust of Diadumenian, r., bareheaded
Inscription: 'Οπελ. 'Αντω. Διαδου. . . . .
Rev.: Bust of Men, r.
Inscription: Σιλλυέων

   Bibliography:
   Lane, II, p. 39, Sillyon 14, and Pl. XII, 1

Weight: 8.88 gr. (Athens)
Illustrated example: Athens

Sillyon 24 Plate L

Obv.: Bust of Diadumenian, r., bareheaded
Inscription: 'Οπελ 'Αντω. Διαδουμενιανὸς Και.
Rev.: Men riding l.
Inscription: Σιλλυέων

   Bibliography:
   Imhoof, *SNR*, 1913, p. 83, no. 236
   SNG Cop., *Lycia*, Pl. 13, no. 447
   Lane, II, p. 39, Sillyon 15 and Pl. XII, 2

Weight: 19.20 gr. (Copenhagen) - 26.60 gr. (Berlin)
Illustrated example: Copenhagen

Sillyon 25 Plate L

Obv.: Bust of Julia Maesa, r.
Inscription: 'Ιουλίαν Μαῖσαν

Rev.: Men riding r.
Inscription: Σιλλυέων

> Bibliography:
> SNG Aulock, Pl. 159, no. 4884
> Lane, II, p. 38, Sillyon 11
> Mary Comstock, Bulletin of the Museum of Fine Arts Boston, 1967, no. 342, p. 171, fig. 17
> Thomas Olive Mabott Coll., New York, 1969, I, no. 1991

Weight: 22.00 (Aulock)
Illustrated example: Mabott

Sillyon 26 Plate L

Obv.: Bust of Elagabalus, r., laureate
Inscription illegible
Rev.: Men standing r. with foot on bucranium
Inscription: Σιλλυέων

> Bibliography:
> Svoronos, *JIAN*, 1903, p. 220, no. 424
> Lane, II, p. 38, Sillyon 9 and Pl. XI, 9

Weight: 5.74 gr. (Athens)
Illustrated example: Athens

Sillyon 27 Plate L

Obv.: Bust of Severus Alexander, r., laureate
Inscription: Αὐ. Και. Αὐρ. Σ. Σ. 'Αλέξανδρος Σεβ.
Rev.: Men standing l. with pine-cone and staff
Inscription: Σιλλυέων

> Bibliography:
> Egger, cat. 41, 1912, Pl. XVII, no. 605
> Egger, cat. 46, 1914, no. 2000

Weight: 24.01 gr. (Budapest)
Illustrated example: Budapest

Sillyon 28 Plate L

Obv.: Bust of Maximinus, r. laureate
Inscription: Μαξιμεῖνος

COINS 143

Rev.: Bust of Men, r., stars on cap
Inscription: Σιλλυέων

> Bibliography:
> *Inv. Wadd.*, *RN*, 1898, p. 41, no. 3535
> Lane, II, p. 39, Sillyon 16 and Pl. XII, 3

Weight: 4.16 gr. (Paris) - 4.57 gr. (Gotha)
Illustrated example: Paris

Sillyon 29 Plate LI

Obv.: Bust of Gordian, r., laureate
Inscription: Αὐ. Κ. Μαρ. 'Αντ. Γορδιανόν
Rev.: Men standing r. with pine-cone and staff, foot on bucranium
Inscription: Σιλλυέων

> Bibliography:
> Svoronos, *JIAN*, 1903, p. 220, no. 427
> Lane, II, p. 39, Sillyon 17 and Pl. XII, 4

Weight: 20.91 gr. (Athens) - 24.98 gr. (Paris)
Illustrated example: Athens

Sillyon 30 Plate LI

Obv.: Bust of Gordian III, r., laureate
Inscription: Αὐ. Κ. Μαρ. 'Αν. Γορδιανόν Σ.
Rev.: Bust of Men, r., with starry cap
Inscription: Σιλλυέων

> Bibliography:
> Waddington, *RN*, 1853, p. 37, no. 3
> Drexler, col. 2720
> *Inv. Wadd.*, *RN*, 1898, p. 41, no. 3536
> Lane II, p. 39, no. 18 and Pl. XII, 5

Weight: 14.15 gr. (Paris)
Illustrated example: Paris

Sillyon 31 Plate LI

Obv.: Bust of Philip II, r., laureate
Inscription: Αὐ. Κ. Μ. 'Ιου. Σεου. Φίλιππος Σ.

Rev.: Bust of Men, r., with starry cap
Inscription: Σιλλυέων

    Bibliography: none

Weight: 18.63 gr. (Paris)
Illustrated example: Paris
Remarks: Apparently intended for the largest denomination of a three denomination series.

Sillyon 32   Plate LI

Obv.: Bust of Philip II, r., laureate
Inscription: Αὐ. Κ. Μ. 'Ιου. Σεου. Φίλιππος Σ.
Rev.: Bust of Men, r., with starry cap
Inscription: Σιλλυέων

    Bibliography:
    Webster, *NC*, 1873, p. 31
    Drexler, col. 2720
    BMC Lycia, p. 168, no. 15 and 15a and Pl. XXIX, 10 (rev. only)
    SNG Aulock, Pl. 159, no. 4886
    Lane, II, p. 39, Sillyon 19

Weight: 7.68 gr.-10.00 gr. (London)
Illustrated example: Aulock

Sillyon 33   Plate LI

Obv.: Bust of Philip II, r., laureate
Inscription: Αὐ. Κ. Μ. 'Ιου. Σεου. Φίλιππος Σ.
Rev.: Bust of Men, r., with starry cap
Inscription: Σιλλυέων

    Bibliography:
    SNG Aulock, Pl. 297, no. 8556

Weight: 3.80 gr. (Aulock) - 4.55 gr. (Aulock)
Illustrated example: Aulock
Remarks: A smaller denomination than the two preceding.

Sillyon 34   Plate LI

Obv.: Bust of Philip II, r., laureate
Inscription: Αὐ. Κ. Μ. ’Ιου. Σεου. Φίλιππος Σε.
Rev.: Men standing r. with staff and pine-cone, foot on bucranium
Inscription: Σιλλυέων

    Bibliography:
    SNG Aulock, Pl. 159, no. 4887
    Lane, II, p. 39, Sillyon 20

Weight: 3.90 gr. (Aulock)
Illustrated example: Aulock

Sillyon 35   Plate LI

Obv.: Bust of Otacilia Severa, r.
Inscription: ... Σευῆρα. ...
Rev.: Men riding l.
Inscription: Σιλλυέων

    Bibliography: none

Weight: 3.42 gr. (Gotha)
Illustrated example: Gotha

Sillyon 36   Plate LI

Obv.: Bust of Valerian, r., laureate
Inscription: Virtually illegible except for I
Rev.: Men riding l.
Inscription: Σιλλυέων

    Bibliography: none

Weight: 35.73 gr. (Berlin)
Illustrated example: Berlin
Remarks: I have kept the attribution made in the Berlin collection, but suspect that we may be dealing merely with a variant of Sillyon 51 (Cornelius Valerianus).

146 COINS

Sillyon 37   Plate LII

Obv.: Bust of Gallienus, r., laureate
Inscription: Αὐτ. Και. Πο. Λ. Γαλλιηνὸ. Σεβ. I
Rev.: Bust of Men, r. Under it, eagle. Stars on cap.
Inscription: Σιλλυέων I (I apparently lacking on some dies)

> Bibliography:
> Waddington, *RN*, 1853, p. 37, no. 5
> Drexler, col. 2720
> *Inv. Wadd.*, *RN*, 1898, p. 42, no. 3541
> Svoronos, *JIAN*, 1903, p. 220, no. 429
> *SNG Cop.*, *Lycia*, Pl. 13, no. 448
> *SNG Aulock*, Pl. 159, no. 4888
> Kraft, Pl. 113, no. 75

Weight: 14.82 gr. (Munich) - 19.78 gr. (Aulock)
Illustrated example: Athens

Sillyon 38   Plate LII

Obv.: Bust of Gallienus, l., laureate, palm branch in field
Inscription: Αὐτ. Και. Π. Λι. Γαλλιηνό.
Rev.: Bust of Men, l.
Inscription: Σιλλυέων

> Bibliography:
> Fiorelli, p. 201, no. 8469 (attributed to Antoninus Pius)
> Svoronos, *JIAN*, 1903, p. 220, no. 428

Weight: 9.27 gr. (Athens) - 11.35 gr. (Naples)
Illustrated example: Athens

Sillyon 39   Plate LII

Obv.: Bust of Gallienus, l., laureate. Palm branch in field.
Inscription: Αὐτ. Και. Π. Λ. Γαλλιηνό.
Rev.: Bust of Men, r., with starry cap
Inscription: Σιλλυέων

> Bibliography:
> Roscher, Pl. Ia, no. 17 (rev. only)
> Drexler, col. 2720
> Imhoof, *Kl. M.*, II, p. 353, no. 19 and Pl. XII, 12
> Lane, II, p. 38, Sillyon 22

Weight: 10.60 gr. (Winterthur) - 20.15 gr. (Berlin)
Illustrated example: Berlin
Remarks: The rev. stands out for its handsomeness among the usually hideous coins of Sillyon from the period of Gallienus.

Sillyon 40   Plate LII

Obv.: Bust of Gallienus, r., laureate
Inscription: Αὐτ. Και. Πο. Λι. Γαλλιηνός Ι
Rev.: Bust of Men, r., globe under bust
Inscription: Σιλλυέων Ι

> Bibliography:
> Imhoof, *Kl. M.*, II, p. 354, Sillyon 20 and Pl. XII, 13 (rev. only)

Weight: 15.25 gr. (Berlin)
Illustrated example: Berlin

Sillyon 41   Plate LII

Obv.: Bust of Gallienus, r., laureate
Inscription: Αὐ. Κ. Π. Λ. Γαλλιηνός
Rev.: Bust of Men, r., nothing under bust
Inscription: Σιλλυέων

> Bibliography:
> Svoronos, *JIAN*, 1903, p. 220, no. 430
> Imhoof-Blumer, *SNR*, 1908, p. 70, Sillyon 3
> Lane, II, p. 39, Sillyon 24 and Pl. XII, 6

Weight: 5.03 gr. (Athens) - 7.40 gr. (Winterthur)
Illustrated example: Athens

Sillyon 42   Plate LII

Obv.: Bust of Gallienus, r., laureate
Inscription: Αὐ. Πο. Λικιν. Γαλλιηνός Ι
Rev.: Bust of Men, r., with starry cap. Nothing under bust.
Inscription: Σιλλυέων Ι

> Bibliography: none

Weight: 14.84 gr. (Brussels)
Illustrated example: Brussels

Sillyon 43   Plate LII

Obv.:   Bust of Gallienus, r., laureate
Inscription: Αὐτ. Και. Πο. Λι. Γαλλιηνός Σεβ. Ι
Rev.:   Men riding r.
Inscription: Σιλλυέων

    Bibliography:
    BMC Lycia, p. 168, no. 17
    SNG Aulock, Pl. 159, no. 4889
    Lane, II, p. 39, Sillyon 25

Weight: 12.07 gr. (London) - 16.62 gr. (Aulock)
Illustrated example: Aulock

Sillyon 44   Plate LII

Obv.:   Facing busts of Gallienus and Salonina r. and l.
Inscription: Αὐ. Κ. Πομ. Λι. Γαλλιηνός . . . . Ι . . . . Κορνηλι
. . . .
Rev.:   Bust of Men, r.
Inscription: Σιλλυέων

    Bibliography:
    SNG Aulock, Pl. 159, no. 4890
    Lane, II, p. 40, Sillyon 28

Weight: 16.11 gr. (London) - 22.45 gr. (Aulock)
Illustrated example: Aulock

Sillyon 45   Plate LIII

Obv.:   Bust of Salonina, r.
Inscription: Κορνηλία Σαλωνῖνα Σεβ. Ι
Rev.:   Bust of Men, r., with starry cap
Inscription: Σιλλυέων

    Bibliography:
    Drexler, col. 2720
    BMC Lycia, p. 298, no. 20a
    Inv. Wadd., *RN*, 1898, p. 42, no. 3542
    SNG Cop., Lycia, Pl. 13, no. 450
    Lane, II, p. 39, Sillyon 26

Weight: 20.24 (London) - 25.73 (Copenhagen)
Illustrated example: Copenhagen

Sillyon 46 Plate LIII

Obv.: Bust of Salonina, r.
Inscription: Κορνηλία Σαλωνῖνα Σε. I
Rev.: Bust of Men, l.
Inscription: Σιλλυέων

    Bibliography: none

Weight: 20.94 gr. (Baldwin's)
Illustrated example: Baldwin's

Sillyon 47 Plate LIII

Obv.: Bust of Salonina, r.
Inscription: Κορνηλία Σαλωνῖνα Σεβ. I
Rev.: Men riding r.
Inscription: Σιλλυέων

    Bibliography:
    Hunt., II, p. 514, no. 2
    Lane, II, p. 39, Sillyon 27 and Pl. XII, 7

Weight: 22.38 gr. (Oxford)
Illustrated example: Oxford

Sillyon 48 Plate LIII

Obv.: Bust of Salonina, r.
Inscription: Κορνηλία Σαλωνῖνα Σεβα. I
Rev.: Men riding r.
Inscription: Σιλλυέων I

    Bibliography: none

Weight: 15.36 gr. (Mossop)
Illustrated example: Mossop collection
Remarks: Apparently intended for a smaller denomination than the preceding, in spite of the I.

Sillyon 49 Plate LIV

Obv.: Bust of Cornelius Valerianus, r., laureate. Eagle under bust.
Inscription: Που. Λικ. Κορ. Οὐαλεριανόν I

Rev.:   Bust of Men, r., with starry cap
Inscription: Σιλλυέων

>Bibliography:
>T. Prowe, NS, 1913, p. 175, no. 62 and Pl. VI
>SNG Aulock, Pl. 159, no. 4891
>Lane, II, p. 40, Sillyon 29

Weight: 17.38 gr. (Budapest) - 20.50 gr. (Munich)
Illustrated example: Budapest

Sillyon 50   Plate LIV

Obv.:   Bust of Cornelius Valerianus, r., laureate. Eagle under bust.
Inscription: Που. Λικ. Κορ. Οὐαλεριανόν Ι
Rev.:   Men riding l.
Inscription: Σιλλυέων

>Bibliography:
>Imhoof-Blumer, Kl. M., II, p. 354, Sillyon 21

Weight: 14.85 gr. (Winterthur) - 22.84 gr. (London)
Illustrated example: Winterthur
Remarks: Imhoof calls the person Saloninus, but reads the titles of Cornelius Valerianus on a very worn coin.

Sillyon 51   Plate LIV

Obv.:   Bust of Cornelius Valerianus, r., laureate. No eagle under bust
Inscription: Και. Πο. Λι. Οὐαλερι. . . .
Rev.:   Men riding l.
Inscription: Σιλλυέων

>Bibliography: none

Weight: 41.88 gr. (Paris)
Illustrated example: Paris

Sillyon 52   Plate LIV

Obv.:   Bust of Saloninus, r., laureate
Inscription: Πο. Λικ. Σαλων. Οὐαλεριανό. Σεβ.

Rev.: Bust of Men r.
Inscription: Σιλλυέων

> Bibliography:
> Drexler, col. 2720
> *Inv. Wadd.*, *RN*, 1898, p. 42, no. 3543
> Svoronos, *JIAN*, 1903, p. 221, no. 431
> Grose, III, p. 265, no. 8932 and Pl. 318.4
> Lane, II, p. 40, Sillyon 30-31 and Pl. XII, 8-9

Weight: 12.50 gr (Oxford) - 18.12 gr. (Cambridge)
Illustrated example: Oxford

Sillyon 53   Plate LV

Obv.: Bust of Aurelian, r., laureate
Inscription: Αὐτ. Λου. Δομι. Αὐρηλιανός I
Rev.: Men riding r.
Inscription: Σιλλυέων Θεοῦ Μηνὸς 'Ασύλου

> Bibliography:
> Imhoof-Blumer, *SNR*, 1908, p. 70, Sillyon 4

Weight: 8.86 gr. (Imhoof) - 9.70 gr. (Athens)
Illustrated example: Athens

Sillyon 54   Plate LV

Obv.: Bust of Aurelian, r., laureate
Inscription: Αὐτ. Λου. Δομι. Αὐρηλιανὸς Σ. I
Rev.: Bust of Men, r.
Inscription: Σιλλυέων Θεοῦ Μηνὸς 'Ασύλου

> Bibliography:
> *BMC Lycia*, p. LXXXVI

Weight: 11.73 gr. (Paris)
Illustrated example: Paris

Galatia 1   Plate LV

Obv.: Bust of Men, r., with starry cap
No inscription
Rev.: Monogram of King Deiotarus between crossed cornucopiae

Bibliography:
Imhoof, *Kl. M.*, II, p. 528, no. 6 and Pl. XX, no. 25
Newell, *RBN*, 1934, p. 5, no. 1 and Pl. I, no. 1
SNG Aulock, Pl. 304, no. 8719
Lane, II, p. 42

Weight: 10.14 gr. (Aulock) - 10.71 gr. (New York)
Illustrated example: Aulock

Galatia 2 Plate LV

Obv.: Bust of Men, l., with starry cap
Inscription: Κοινὸν Γαλατῶν
Rev.: Hexastyle temple
Inscription: Σεβαστῶν

Bibliography:
Imhoof, *Gr. M.*, p. 750, no. 746 and Pl. XIII, 6
Roscher, Pl. Ia, no. 8 (Obv. only)
Drexler, col. 2727
Inv. Wadd., *RN*, 1898, p. 556, no. 6591
SNG Aulock, Pl. 304, no. 8721
Lane, II, p. 41, Ancyra 10 and Pl. XIII, 4

Weight: 5.88 gr. (Berlin) - 8.42 gr. (Paris)
Illustrated example: Berlin

Galatia 3 Plate LV

Obv.: Bust of Nerva, r., laureate
Inscription: Αὐτο Νέρουας Καῖσαρ Σεβαστός
Rev.: Men standing l., with patera and pine-cone

Inscription: Ἐπὶ Τ. Πομπονίου Βάσσου (with variations)

Bibliography:
Drexler, col. 2727
Inv. Wadd., *RN*, 1898, p. 566, no. 6595
SNG Aulock, Pl. 304, no. 8722
SNG Fitz., Pl. 113, no. 5385
Lane, II, p. 40, Ancyra 2 and Pl. XIII, no. 1; III, p. 105, no. 19

Weight: 7.01 gr. (Oxford) - 13.06 gr. (Cambridge)
Illustrated example: Istanbul

Galatia 4 Plate LV

Obv.: Bust of Trajan, r., laureate
Inscription: Αὐτ. Νερ. Τραιανὸς Καῖσαρ Σεβ.
Rev.: Men standing l. with patera and pine-cone
Inscription: 'Επὶ Βάσσου Κοινὸν Γαλατίας (very variable)

> Bibliography:
> Drexler, col. 2727
> *BMC Galatia*, p. 6, no. 6, and Pl. I, 11 (rev. only); p. 6, no. 7
> *Inv. Wadd.*, *RN* 1898, p. 566, no. 6600 and Pl. XV, 21 (rev. only)
> Imhoof, *Kl. M.*, I, p. 495, Ankyra 3
> J. Scholz, *NZ*, 1910, 1910, p. 27, no. 154
> *SNG Cop., Cyprus*, Pl. 3, no. 104
> Lane, II, p. 40, Ancyra 3

Weight: 4.95 gr. (Imhoof) - 13.25 gr. (London)
Illustrated example: Missouri

Galatia 5 Plate LV

Obv.: Bust of Trajan, r., laureate
Inscription: Αὐτ. Νερ. Τραιανός Καῖσαρ Σεβ.
Rev.: Men standing l. with patera and pine-cone
Inscription: 'Επὶ Βάσσου Κοινὸν Γαλατίας

> Bibliography: none

Weight: 22.67 gr. (Paris)
Illustrated example: Paris
Remarks: Although the basic type of this coin is highly variable in weight, this definitely looks like a double denomination, and hence I have separated it from the others.

Galatia 6 Plate LV

Obv.: Bust of Trajan, r., radiate
Inscription: Αὐ. Νερ. Τραιανὸς Σε. Γ.
Rev.: Men standing l. with patera and pine-cone
Inscription: Κοινὸν Γαλατίας ἐπὶ Πομ. Βάσσου

> Bibliography:
> *Inv. Wadd.*, *RN*, 1898, p. 566, no. 6601
> *SNG Fitz.*, Pl. 113, no. 5389
> Lane, II, p. 105, no. 21

Weight: 11.42 gr. (Paris) - 17.30 gr. (Cambridge)
Illustrated example: Cambridge

Galatia 7   Plate LV

Obv.:   Bust of Trajan, r., laureate
Inscription: Αὐτ. Νερ. Τραιανὸς Καῖσαρ Σε. Γ.
Rev.:   Men with patera and pine-cone, standing in distyle temple, seen in 3/4 view to l.
Inscription: Κοινὸν Γαλατίας ἐπὶ Πομπωνίου Βάσσου

> Bibliography:
> Roscher, Pl. Ib, 15 (rev. only)
> Drexler, col. 2727
> *Inv. Wadd., RN* 1898, p. 566, no. 6596
> D. Krencker and M. Schede, *Der Tempel in Ankara*, Berlin 1936, Pl. XLV F (rev. only)
> *SNG Fitz.*, Pl. 113, no. 5387
> Lane, II, p. 41, Ancyra 12 and III, p. 105, no. 20

Weight: 18.68 gr. (Paris) - 22.79 gr. (Cambridge)
Illustrated example: Cambridge

Galatia 8   Plate LVI

Obv.:   Bust of Trajan, r., laureate
Inscription: Νερ. Τραιανὸς Καῖσαρ Σε.
Rev.:   Men standing as before, but temple to r.
Inscription: .... ἐπὶ Βάσσου

> Bibliography: none

Weight: 20.32 gr. (Paris) - 21.28 gr. (London)
Illustrated example: Paris

Ancyra 1   Plate LVI

Obv.:   Bust of Men, r.
No inscription
Rev.:   Inscription arranged in four lines: Σεβαστηνῶν Τεκτοσάγων

> Bibliography:
> Imhoof, *Gr. M.*, p. 750, no. 747

Drexler, col. 2727
Inv. Wadd., *RN*, 1898, p. 566, no. 6604
Lane, II, p. 41, Ancyra 11 and Pl. XIII, 5

Weight: 3.56 gr. (Paris) - 4.19 gr. (Gotha)
Illustrated example: Paris

Ancyra 2   Plate LVI

Obv.: Bust of Titus, r., laureate
Inscription: Αὐ. Καῖσαρ Τῖτος Σεβαστοῦ Υἱός (with variations)
Rev.: Men standing l. holding patera, l. hand at side
Inscription: Σεβαστηνῶν Τεκτοσάγων

> Bibliography:
> Imhoof, *MG*, p. 415, no. 174
> Roscher, Pl. Ia, 19 (rev. only)
> Drexler, col. 2727
> *BMC Galatia*, p. 8, no. 1 and Pl. II, no. 1 (rev. only)
> *Inv. Wadd.*, *RN*, 1898, p. 567, no. 6605
> *Hunt.*, II, p. 569, no. 2
> *SNG Cop.*, *Cyprus*, Pl. 4, no. 107
> Lane, II, p. 40, Ancyra 1

Weight: 8.73 gr. (Paris) - 13.77 gr. (Copenhagen)
Illustrated example: Copenhagen

Ancyra 3   Plate LVI

Obv.: Bust of Antinous r.
Inscription: Ἀντίνοος Θεός
Rev.: Men standing l. holding anchor
Inscription: Ἰούλιος Σατορνῖνος Ἀνκυρανοῖς

> Bibliography:
> *Inv. Wadd.*, *RN*, 1898, p. 567, no. 6607 and Pl. XV, 23
> *SNG Cop.*, *Cyprus*, Pl. 4, no. 108
> M. Grant, *Roman History from Coins*, Pl. XXX, no. 4
> Lane, II, p. 40, Ancyra 4
> Niggeler, II, p. 19, no. 655 and Pl. 7

Weight: 23.67 gr. (London) - 26.75 gr. (Niggeler)
Illustrated example: Niggeler

Ancyra 4 Plate LVI

Obv.: Bust of Antoninus Pius, r., laureate
Inscription: 'Αντωνεῖνος ......
Rev.: Men standing l. holding staff and pine-cone (?)
Inscription: 'Η Μητρόπολις τῆς Γαλατίας "Ανκυρα

> Bibliography:
> Drexler, col. 2726
> *Inv. Wadd.*, *RN*, 1898, p. 567, no. 6608
> Lane, II, p. 40, Ancyra 5 and Pl. XIII, 2

Weight: 23.50 gr. (Leningrad) - 23.51 gr. (Paris)
Illustrated example: Leningrad

Ancyra 5 Plate LVI

Obv.: Bust of Faustina, jr., r.
Inscription: Φαυστεῖνα Σεβαστή
Rev.: Men standing l. with anchor
Inscription: Μητρο. 'Ανκύρας

> Bibliography:
> Roscher, Pl. Ia, no. 18 (rev. only)
> Drexler, col. 2726
> *Inv. Wadd.*, *RN*, 1898, p. 567, no. 6610
> *BMC Galatia*, p. 9, no. 8 and Pl. II, 3 (rev. only)

Weight: 7.26 gr. (Istanbul) - 10.10 gr. (Munich)
Illustrated example: Istanbul
Remarks: Although not so described in the catalogue of the Waddington collection, the Paris example also, if seen clearly, shows an anchor.

Ancyra 6 Plate LVII

Obv.: Bust of Septimius Severus, r., laureate, with ornamented cuirass
Inscription: Σεουῆρος Αὐγοῦστος
Rev.: Men standing l., holding patera over flaming altar. Cock in front of altar, short staff in Men's hand. Military costume.
Inscription: Μητροπ. 'Ανκύρας

Bibliography:
Drexler, col. 2726
BMC Galatia, p. 11, no. 12 and Pl. II, 5 (rev. only)

Weight: 17.19 gr. (London)
Illustrated example: London

Ancyra 7   Plate LVII

Obv.: Bust of Caracalla, r., laureate
Inscription: Αὐτ. Κ. Μ. Αὐρ. Μ. ’Αντωνεῖνος Αὐτο.
Rev.: Men standing l. with Nike, arm resting on a column, also with spear, bucranium, and cock (Antiochene attributes)
Inscription: Μητροπόλεως ’Ανκύρας

Bibliography:
Drexler, col. 2726
Weber, III, ii, p. 699, no. 7771 and Pl. 282
Lane, II, p. 40, Ancyra 8

Weight: 15.79 gr. (Paris) - 18.46 gr. (London)
Illustrated example: Weber

Ancyra 8   Plate LVII

Obv.: Bust of Caracalla, r., laureate
Inscription: Αὐρ. . . . . ’Αντωνεῖνος Αὐτο.
Rev.: Men standing l. with patera and staff
Inscription: Μητροπόλεως ’Ανκύρας

Bibliography: none

Weight: 14.56 gr. (New York)
Illustrated example: New York

Ancyra 9   Plate LVII

Obv.: Bust of Caracalla, r., laureate, slightly bearded
Inscription: Αὐτ. Κ. Μ. Αὐρ. ’Αντωνεῖνος Αὐγ.
Rev.: Bust of Men, r., with starry cap
Inscription: Μητροπ. ’Ανκύρας

Bibliography:
Drexler, col. 2726
Imhoof, *Kl. M.*, p. 496, no. 6

Weight: 12.06 gr. (Berlin)
Illustrated example: Berlin

Ancyra 10 Plate LVII

Obv.: Bust of Geta, r., laureate
Inscription: Αὐτ. . . . . Γέτας Αὐ.
Rev.: Men standing r. with Antiochene attributes
Inscription: 'Ανκύρας Μητροπο. . . . .

> Bibliography:
> von Rauch, *Berliner Blätter für Münz-, Siegel-, und Wappenkunde*, 1871-3, p. 133, no. 13
> Drexler, col. 2727

Weight: 14.98 gr. (Berlin)
Illustrated example: Berlin

Ancyra 11 Plate LVII

Obv.: Bust of Geta, r., laureate
Inscription: Σεπ. Γέτας
Rev.: Men standing l., holding staff, and patera over altar
Inscription: Μητροπ. 'Ανκύρας

> Bibliography: none

Weight: 17.52 gr. (Evelpides)
Illustrated example: Evelpides

Ancyra 12 Plate LVII

Obv.: Bust of Elagabalus, l., laureate, holding shield and spear
Inscription: 'Αντωνῖνος Αὐγοῦστος
Rev.: Men standing l., holding patera over flaming altar
Inscription: Μητροπο. 'Ανκύρας

> Bibliography:
> Imhoof, *Kl. M.*, p. 495, Ancyra 2
> *SNG Cop., Cyprus*, Pl. 4, no. 119

Weight: 14.09 gr. (Copenhagen)
Illustrated example: Copenhagen

Ancyra 13 Plate LVII

Obv.: Bust of Valerian, r., radiate
Inscription: Γ. Πουβ. Λικ. Οὐαλεριανὸς Σεβ. (with variations)
Rev.: Men standing l. with Antiochene attributes
Inscription: 'Ἀνκύρας Μητροπόλεως β' Ν[εωκορίας]

    Bibliography:
    Drexler, col. 2727
    Lane, II, p. 40, Ancyra 9 and Pl. XIII, 3
    SNG Aulock, p. 1, 213, no. 6188

Weight: 9.72 gr. (New York, damaged) - 11.14 gr. (Aulock)
Illustrated example: Aulock

Ancyra 14 Plate LVII

Obv.: Bust of Salonina, r., with diadem
Inscription: Κορ. Σαλωνεῖνα Σεβ.
Rev.: Men standing l. with patera, foot on bucranium
Inscription: 'Ἀνκύρας Μητροπόλεως β' Ν[εωκορίας]

    Bibliography:
    Niggeler, II, p. 19, no. 656 and Pl. 7

Weight: 12.91 gr. (Niggeler)
Illustrated example: Niggeler

Ancyra 15 Plate LVII

Obv.: Bust of Salonina, r., with diadem
Inscription: Κορνη. Σαλωνεῖ...
Rev.: Men standing r. with Antiochene attributes
Inscription: 'Ἀνκύρας Μητροπόλεως β' Ν[εωκορίας]

    Bibliography:
    SNG Aulock, Pl. 213, no. 6201

Weight: 8.18 gr. (Aulock)
Illustrated example: Aulock

Uncertain, perhaps Ancyra   Plate LVIII

Obv.: Bust of Galba, r., bareheaded
Inscription: Γάλβας Αὐτοκράτωρ Καῖσαρ Σεβαστός
Rev.: Men standing l. with patera and pine-cone
Inscription: Σέρουιος Γάλβας Σεβαστός

>Bibliography:
>Perdrizet, *BCH*, 1896, p. 73, and fig. 4
>Roscher, in note to Drexler, col. 2994 and fig. 3
>Imhoof, *Kl. M.*, II, p. 495, Ancyra 1 and Pl. XIX, 7
>*Hunt.*, II, p. 567, Galatia 1 and Pl. LXI, 21
>*SNG Fitz.*, Pl. 113, no. 5383
>Lane, II, p. 41, Ancyra 13; III, p. 105, no. 18

Weight: 11.49 gr. (London) - 15.63 gr. (Cambridge)
Illustrated example: Cambridge
Remarks: On the basis of the representation (Men holding both patera and pine-cone) this coin has generally been attributed to Ancyra or to the Koinon of the Galatians. The puzzling reverse inscription has been held to indicate that the emperor is being identified with Men. The present author does not feel that either assumption is necessarily justified. Cf. the provincial issues of Lycia under Claudius, on which the emperor's titles are continued on the rev., with representation of various divinities.

Germe 1   Plate LVIII

Obv.: Bust of Commodus, r., laureate
Inscription: Imp. Com. Antonin
Rev.: Bust of Men, r.
Inscription: Co. Germa

>Bibliography:
>H. von Aulock, *Istanbuler Mitteilungen*, 1968, p. 236, no. 15 and Pl. 69

Weight: 4.50 gr. (Paris)
Illustrated example: Paris

Pessinus 1   Plate LVIII

Obv.: Bust of Men, r., with starry cap
No inscription

Rev.: Humped bull, l.
Inscription: Μητρὸς Θεῶν Πεσσινείας

    Bibliography:
    Imhoof, *Gr. M.*, p. 752, nos. 753-4 and Pl. XIII, no. 11
    Drexler, col. 2727-8
    Lane, II, p. 41, Pessinus 1

Weight: 7.45 gr.-9.81 gr. (Paris)
Illustrated example: Imhoof
Remarks: One Paris example has $\overset{*}{\smile}$ in field.

Pessinus 2   Plate LVIII

Obv.: Bust of Men, r.
Inscription: Πεσσινουντίων counterclockwise
Rev.: Bust of Annius Afrinus, r.
Inscription: ῎Αννιος ᾽Αφρῖνος counterclockwise

    Bibliography: none

Weight: 2.85 gr. (Munich) - 2.87 gr. (Berlin)
Illustrated example: Munich

Pessinus 3   Plate LVIII

Obv.: Bust of Antoninus Pius, r., laureate
Inscription: Αὐτοκρα. Και. ᾽Αδρι. ᾽Αντωνεῖνος (with variations)
Rev.: Men standing l. with staff and patera. This patera is held over an altar.
Inscription: Γαλ. Τολισ. Πεσσινουντέων

    Bibliography:
    Drexler, col. 2728
    Inv. Wadd., *RN*, 1898, no. 6655
    Lane, II, Pessinus 2, Pl. XIII, 6

Weight: 9.35 gr. (Vienna) - 12.67 gr. (New York)
Illustrated example: New York

Pessinus 4   Plate LVIII

Obv.: Bust of Caracalla, l. laureate
Inscription: ᾽Αντωνεῖνος Αὐγοῦστος

Rev.: Men standing l. with patera, fold of clothing in lowered l. hand
Inscription: Πεσσινουντίων

> Bibliography: none

Weight: 12.02 gr. (Berlin)
Illustrated example: Berlin

Laodiceia ad Libanum 1   Plate LIX

Obv.: Bust of Septimius Severus, r., laureate
Inscription: Αὐτ. Κ. Λ. Σεπ. Σεουῆρος (with variations)
Rev.: Men standing l., holding horse l. by bridle
Inscription: Λαοδικ. πρὸς Λιβάνῳ Μήν.

> Bibliography:
> De Saulcy, *Numismatique de la Terre Sainte*, Paris 1874, p. 4, no. 1; and no. 2, Pl. I, 1; no. 3
> Drexler, col. 2728
> *Hunt.*, III, p. 22, Laodiceia 1 and Pl. LXXV, 5 (rev. only)

Weight: 7.98 gr. (Paris) - 16.24 gr. (New York)
Illustrated example: New York

Laodiceia ad Libanum 2   Plate LIX

Obv.: Bust of Caracalla, r., bearded, laureate
Inscription: ’Α. Κ. Μ. Αὐρ. ’Αντωνῖνος
Rev.: Men standing l., holding horse l. by bridle
Inscription: Λαοδικ. πρὸς Λιβάνῳ Μήν

> Bibliography:
> De Saulcy, *Numismatique de la Terre Sainte*, p. 4, no. 1 and Pl. I, no. 2; p. 4, no. 2; p. 5, no. 5
> Drexler, col. 2728
> *SNG Cop.*, *Syria: Cities*, Pl. 12, no. 445
> Lane, II, p. 42, Laodiceia 2

Weight: 6.98 gr. (Paris) - 10.89 gr. (Paris)
Illustrated example: Copenhagen

COINS 163

Laodiceia ad Libanum 3   Plate LIX

Obv.: Bust of Caracalla, r., laureate, unbearded
Inscription illegible
Rev.: Men standing l., holding horse l. by bridle, also holding a torch in l. hand
Inscription: Λαοδικεία τῇ πό[λει...] (?)
    Bibliography: none
Weight: 15.00 gr. (Paris)
Illustrated example: Jerusalem, Studium Biblicum Fransiscanum

Laodiceia ad Libanum 4   Plate LIX

Obv.: Bust of Macrinus, r., laureate
Inscription illegible
Rev.: Men standing l., holding horse l. by bridle, also holding torch in l. hand
Inscription: ..... Μήν
    Bibliography: none
Weight: 16.98 gr. (Paris)
Illustrated example: M. Rozenberger Coll., Jerusalem

Imperial Cistophori   Plate LIX

Obv.: Bust of Hadrian, r., bareheaded
Inscription: Hadrianus Augustus P. P.
Rev.: Men standing l. with patera and staff
Inscription: Cos. III
    Bibliography:
    Regling, *Nysa*, p. 81
    H. Mattingly and E. Sydenham, *Roman Imperial Coinage*, II (London, 1926), p. 401, no. 502
    Coins of the Roman Empire in the British Museum, III (1936), p. 388, no. 1070, and Pl. 73, no. 3
Weight: 10.63 gr. (London)
Illustrated example: London
Remarks: The only silver coin with Men known to me. Provides a parallel for the only other Men-coin not bound to a specific location, that of Galba sometimes attributed to Ancyra.

GEMS

G 1   Plate LX

Representation: Men standing, head frontal, staff in right hand, pine-cone in left
Location: Paris

> Bibliography:
> Perdrizet, *BCH*, 20, 1896, p. 55, fig. 1
> Daremberg-Saglio, *Dictionnaire des Antiquités*, III, p. 1393, fig. 4663
> S. Reinach, *Pierres Gravées des Collections Marlborough et d'Orleans ......*, Paris, 1895, Pl. 88, no. 59
> Chabouillet, *Catalogue des camees et Pierres Gravées de la Bibliothèque Imperiale*, Paris, 1858, p. 264, no. 2033
> Lane, III, p. 100, no. 1
> Richter, *Engraved Gems of the Romans*, 1971, p. 49, no. 210
> Drexler, col. 2746

Dimensions: 18 × 14 mm

G 2   Plate LX

Representation: Men standing r. with staff and pine-cone, foot on bucranium
Location: Paris

> Bibliography:
> Chabouillet, *op. cit.*, p. 264, no. 2034
> Perdrizet, *BCH*, 20, 1896, p. 103, fig. 7
> Lane, III, p. 100, no. 2 and Pl. XXV, no. 2
> Drexler, col. 2746

Dimensions: unavailable

G 3   Plate LX

Representation: Head of Men, r., cap laureate, crescent visible only front and back
Location: London

> Bibliography:
> H. B. Walters, *British Museum Catalogue of Engraved Gems, Greek, Etruscan, and Roman*, 2nd ed., 1926 no. 1672 and Pl. XXII

Drexler, col. 2745, fig. 11
Lane, III, p. 100, no. 3
King, *Antique Gems and Rings*, 2, Pl. 16, no. 4

Dimensions: 19 × 15 mm

Remarks: References to earlier editions of British Museum and Metropolitan Museum catalogues are not given. They can be found from 2nd eds.

G 4   Plate LX

Representation: Head of Men, r., crescent all the way P underneath. Star in field

Location: London

> Bibliography:
> Walters, *op. cit.*, no. 1673
> Lane, III, p. 100, no. 4 and Pl. XXV, 3
> Drexler, col. 2745

Dimensions: 15 × 13 mm

G 5   Plate LX

Representation: Head of Men, r., crudely rendered crescent front and back

Location: New York

> Bibliography:
> G. M. A. Richter, *Catalogue of Engraved Gems, Greek, Etruscan, and Roman, in the Metropolitan Museum*, New York, 2nd ed., Rome, 1956, no. 378, and Pl. XLVIII
> Lane, III, p. 100, no. 5

Dimensions: 14 mm

G 6   Plate LX

Representation: Men standing frontally with Antiochene attributes (but without rooster)

Location: Latour Maubourg Coll.

> Bibliography:
> A. Furtwängler, *Die Antiken Gemmen*, Leipzig and Berlin, 1900, Pl. LXIV, no. 64

Bulletino dell'Instituto, 1839, p. 106, no. 80
Lane, III, p. 100, n . 6

Dimensions: 11 × 10 mm

G 7   Plate LX

Representation: Men standing left holding indistinct object, bare from waist up, crescent behind shoulders. The Phrygian cap seems to have a brim.

Location: Berlin

> Bibliography:
> A. Furtwängler, *Beschreibung der geschnittenen Steine im Antiquarium*, Berlin, 1896, no. 2934
> E. H. Toelken, *Erklärendes Verzeichnis der antiken vertieft geschnittenen Steine*, Berlin, 1835, p. 239, no. 1403
> Lane, III, p. 100, no. 7

Dimensions: 14 × 11 mm

G 8   Plate LX

Representation: Men standing l., holding patera and pine cone(?). In front, altar; in back, rooster.

Location: Berlin

> Bibliography:
> Furtwängler, *Beschreibung*, no. 6794
> Toelken, *op. cit.*, p. 240, no. 1404
> Lane, III, p. 101, no. 8

Dimensions: 19 × 14 mm

G 9   Plate LXI

Representation: Head of Men, r., Phrygian cap, crescent at neck
Location: Florence

> Bibliography:
> S. Reinach, *op. cit.*, Pl. 58, no. II 40[1]
> Lane, II, p. 101, no. 9
> Drexler, col. 2745
> Milani, *Museo italiano di antichita classica*, I, 1884, p. 132, no. 11
> Gori, *Museum Florentinum, Gemmae antiquae*, 1731-2, vol. II, p. 40, no. 1

Dimensions: 13 × 10 mm

GEMS

G 10 Plate LXI

Representation: Head of Men, l., with Phrygian cap and crescent
Location: Athens

> Bibliography:
> Lane, III, p. 101, no. 11 and Pl. XXV, no. 4

Dimensions: 14 × 11 mm

G 11 Plate LXI

Representation: Head of Men, r., crescent at neck. No wreath on cap.
Location: Bloomington, Indiana

> Bibliography:
> *A Selection of Gems from the Collection of Burton Y. Berry*, Bloomington, 1965, no. 19
> Lane, III, p. 101, no. 10
> *Ancient Gems from the Collection of Burton Y. Berry*, Bloomington, 1969, no. 29

Dimensions: 18 × 13 mm

G 12 Plate LXI

Representation: Men standing l., holding a patera. In front, altar; in back, rooster.
Location: Bloomington, Indiana

> Bibliography:
> *Ancient Gems from the Collection of Burton Y. Berry*, Bloomington, 1969, no. 51

Dimensions: 12 × 10 mm

G 13 Plate LXI

Representation: Zeus seated holding a statue of Nike. To his r., Hermes. To his l., a bust of Men.
Location: Bloomington, Indiana

> Bibliography:
> *Ancient Gems from the Collection of Burton Y. Berry*, Bloomington, 1969, no. 105

Dimensions: 15 × 12 mm

G 14   Plate LXII

Representation: Bust of Men, r., with crescent at neck. No wreath on cap.
Location: ?

>Bibliography:
>J. B. Passerius, *Novus Thesaurus Gemmarum Veterum*, I, Rome, 1781, Pl. 34
>Lane, III, p. 101, no. 12

Dimensions: unknown

G 15   Plate LXIII

Representation: Men standing l. without attributes. To l. altar, to r., rooster.
Location: ?

>Bibliography:
>J. B. Passerius, *Novus Thesaurus Gemmarum Veterum*, I, Rome, 1781, Pl. 35
>Drexler, col. 2746
>Lane, III, p. 101, no. 13

Dimensions: unknown

G 16   Plate LXIV

Representation: Bust of Men, r., stars on cap
Location: Naples

>Bibliography:
>A. M. Migliari, *Annali dell'Instituto*, 1843, pp. 392-3, Pl. O, no. 2
>Drexler, col. 2745
>Visconti, *Opere Varie*, II, Milan, 1829, p. 352, no. 35, and p. 244, no. 288 (same item?)
>Lane, III, p. 101, no. 14

Dimensions: unavailable

G 17   Plate LXIV

Representation: Men standing frontally with globe (pine-cone?) in r. hand
Inscription: Μεὶς Γοισηανός

On rev.: Same scene, but without inscription.
Location: Bibliothèque Nationale, Paris
> Bibliography:
> A. de Ridder, *Collection de Clerq*, VII, 2, *Les Pierres Gravées*, Paris, 1911, no. 3523
> Lane, III, p. 101, no. 15

Dimensions: 9 × 12 mm

Remarks: The provenience of this gem is said to be Saita (Sidon). I have been unable to track down the items listed by Drexler, from *Museo di Denh*, and from Cavedoni, Bull. dell' Instituto, 1841, p. 112.

G 18   Plate LXIV

Representation: Bust of Men, l.
Location: Author's private possession, from Hon. Burton Y. Berry
> Bibliography: none

Dimensions: 11 × 8 mm

G 19   Plate LXIV

Representation: Men standing r. holding staff and patera (?) out of which a libation is being poured. The editors describe this latter attribute as a cornucopia, and although I do not exclude this interpretation, it seems unusual in Men-iconography
Location: Munich
> Bibliography:
> *Antike Gemmen in Deutschen Sammlungen*, I, i, no. 422 and Pl. 48

Dimensions: 12.7 × 9.6 mm; thickness 3.1 mm

Finally we should claim for Men the famous silver plate from the Hildesheim Treasure, generally dated to the first century B.C., and discovered in 1868. Although this plate is generally said to portray Attis, it agrees with representations of Men in all iconographical details. A photograph is given at the end of the plates.

> Select Bibliography:
> E. Pernice and F. Winter, *Der Hildesheimer Silberfund*, Berlin, 1901
> U. Gehrig, *Hildesheimer Silberfund*, Berlin, 1967, Pl. 13.

Diameter: 18.9 cm.; height, 4.4 cm.; weight 339.13 gr.

ADDENDA AND CORRIGENDA TO VOLUME I*

A. CORRIGENDA

In spite of my best efforts, there remained a number of typographical errors even in the final version of the first volume of *Corpus Monumentorum Religionis Dei Menis*. Most of these are minor, and will easily be corrected by the reader; but I would like here to list those which are of more consequence, and may cause trouble for the reader:

---

* At Professor Vermaseren's suggestion I address myself here to the rather annoying review of vol. I by Jean Pouilloux, which appeared, *REA*, LXXIV, 1972, pp. 367-368. Some of the detailed criticisms of my book are simply wrong. For instance, I am blamed for having given line drawings of items 7, 21, 51, 77, 133, 171, 175, and 177, instead of photographs, when the monuments are still accessible. In fact, nos. 51, 77, 133, and 171, are to the best of my knowledge not accessible. I have in my possession a photograph of no. 21, but the letters are so faint that it would have lent no aid to anyone, so gave the line-drawing by preference. That leaves the criticism valid only for nos. 7, 175, and 177, at most.

Secondly, M. Pouilloux faults my book for not mentioning the monument published by Miss C. H. E. Haspels, on p. 167 of her generally very informative book, *The Highlands of Phrygia*. In point of fact, this monument (which, incidentally, M. Pouilloux seems to conflate with another monument published by Miss Haspels on p. 200 of the same work) neither contains the name of Men nor conforms to his iconography. Miss Haspels is almost certainly wrong in her attribution, and M. Pouilloux should have recognized it.

After this display, it is disconcerting in the next paragraph to find myself faulted for lack of "efforts critiques." M. Pouilloux is unhappy that I published Hicks' text of no. 15, which he finds incomprehensible. Now the end of no. 15 is indeed puzzling, but it seems to me irresponsible to try to wish it out of existence just because one does not understand it. By that process, much of the evidence for this cult could be wished out of existence.

Mostly, however, M. Pouilloux' unhappiness rests on the fact that I did not undertake a full interpretation of the monuments along with their presentation in volume I. Indeed, except for a few brief remarks, mostly original with myself, I have deliberately postponed discussion and interpretation for volume III, where I will handle it as satisfactorily as I am able. I can only counsel patience.

To give the devil his due, there are a couple of valid remarks in Pouilloux' review. Firstly, it would have been more helpful to the reader had I numbered the lines of the inscriptions. Secondly, I have been inconsistent in whether or not I capitalized incomprehensible portions of inscriptions, following too much the example of my sources, themselves inconsistent. I will try to do better on both scores in the future.

no. 20:   For Cilvastion(o) read Cilvastian(o)
no. 41:   Delete α after]
no. 43:   For ἀχαριατίαν read ἀχαριστίαν
no. 47:   For ἐμαυτὸν read ἐμαυτὴν
no. 62:   Lemma: For Kavakh, read Kavaklı
no. 169:   For Λό[μ]νον read Δό[μ]νον
no. 190:   For Κλαύδιος, read Καισίδιος.
no. 195b: Remove the dot from under the gamma of Γάμος
no. 256:   For *Antonis*, read *Antonia*.
no. 289:   For τεκμορεύσαος read τεκμορεύσασα
no. D5:   In the first line of discussion, for *amend*, read *emend*.
Plate CV: In caption, for A 1 read AD 1

B. ADDENDA TO ITEMS INCLUDED IN THE FIRST VOLUME OF THE *CORPUS*

Here I propose to list what seems to me the most significant bibliographical references to items listed in the *Corpus*-references which either have appeared since its publication, or were overlooked by or unavailable to me at the time I wrote it. I do not profess to be complete. Those references which concern themselves only in passing or in general terms with the material will be mentioned in the volume of conclusions, if they have anything to contribute to the discussion. Only fairly specific items are treated here.

No. 2 is now in the Museum of Fine Arts, Boston.
No. 13 is published by F. Sokolowski, *Lois Sacrées des Cités Grecques*, Paris, 1969, no. 55 with an interesting commentary and many bibliographical references. (I am indebted for this reference to the valuable review of my first volume by Giovanni Geraci in *Rivista Storica dell' Antichità*, 1972, pp. 275-279).
No. 16 is published by L. Vidman, *Sylloge inscriptionium religionis Isiacae et Sarapiacae* (Berlin, 1969), no. 176, and discussed, *Isis und Sarapis bei den Griechen und Römern* (Berlin, 1970) pp. 66-67.
In no. 23, Geraci suggests the filling of the lacuna in the last line with [Flavio]. He also suggests that in the whole set of Latin inscriptions the abbreviation V C be taken as V(ir) C(larissimus)

rather than V(ir) C(onsularis). I am very glad to have these suggestions, as I am not at home in late Latin epigraphy.

No. 50 is discussed by J. L. Robert, *REG*, 84, 1971, p. 498.

No. 53 is published by F. Sokolowski, *Lois Sacrées de l'Asie Mineure*, Paris, 1955, no. 19, with interesting commentary, but with the date off by one year.

No. 75 is discussed by H. W. Pleket, *Mnemosyne*, 1970, p. 192-195 with particular reference to the word σημαῖα.

No. 111 is discussed by Mara Bonfioli and Silvio Panciera in *Pontificia Accademia Romana di Archeologia, Rendiconti*, 44, 1971-72, p. 199. They are concerned with the possibility of Christianity in the household of the descendentsa of Sergius Paulus, the proconsul of Cyprus who listened to St. Paul preaching, according to *Acts*, 13, 12. Their conclusions are basically negative.

No. 163 not illustrated in vol. I, is illustrated by B. Levick, *JHS*, 91, 1971, Pl. XI.

No. 195 is discussed by W. M. Ramsay, *The Athenaeum*, July 13, 1912, pp. 45-46. In this he makes clear that our nos. 190 and 195b are actually identical, 195b being his reinterpretation of 190.

No. 255 is discussed by B. Levick, *JHS*, 91, 1971, 80 ff.

No. 264 is discussed by Ramsay, *The Athenaeum*, Sept. 7, 1912, pp. 252-3. Here he makes clear that this piece, and presumably also nos. 260-63, were found in 1912 in the area of the sanctuary.

Nos. 283 and 290 are discussed by B. Levick and A. M. Davis in *Classical Review*, 1971, pp. 162-166, as to the word κοπτοπώλης or "confectioner". The word συμμαρούδης is interpreted as Latin *summa rudis*, "fencing master".

C. MATERIAL NOT LISTED IN THE FIRST VOLUME OF
THE *CORPUS*

I. *New Material*

Tosuntaşı

(14 km. SSW of Bozkır, Turkey)

A 5. A bossed rectangular block of limestone found by T. Mitford in the local cemetery on August 13 or 14, 1966.

Dimensions: Height 49 cm., width 1.05 m., thickness 65 cm., letters 3.5 to 3 cm.

> Bibliography: G. E. Bean and T. B. Mitford, *Journeys in Rough Cilicia, 1964-1968* (Österreichische Akademie der Wissenschaften, Phil.-Hist. Klasse, Denkschriften, 102, 1970), p. 118, no. 105 and Photograph 90.

The stone bears the following inscription:

['Ο]ρκίσζω Μῆνα καταχθόνιον καὶ οὐράνιον
vac. μηθένα δόλον τῷ ἔργῳ (sc. γενέσθαι)

Comana Cappadociae: Şar, Turkey

A 6. Round altar of pink marble, decorated with scrolls on the sides.
Dimensions: Height 35 mm., diameter 18 mm, letters 2 mm.

> Bibliography: R. F. Harper, *Anatolian Studies*, XXII, 1972, p. 225, no. 3, 10 and fig. 1, 2.

The stone bears the following inscription:

Κυρίῳ Μηνὶ Ἡλιόδωρος
Δημητρίου νεωκόρος
ὑπὲρ τῆς Διοδώρου
Γορδίου τοῦ ἱερέως
σωτηρίας

These two inscriptions are interesting in that they show the presence of the Men-cult further to the South-East than previously attested.

Kalburcu

Vicinity of *Nicomedeia*: Izmit, Turkey

A 7. Profiled basis (altar?) of limestone, known since 1974.
Dimensions: Height 1.16 m.; width 39 cm.; thickness 39 cm.; letters 5 cm.

> Bibliography: S. Şahin, *Neufunde von Antiken Inscriften in Nikomedeia (Izmit) und in der Umgebung der Stadt* (Dissertation, Münster), 1974, p. 121, no. 66.

The stone bears the following inscription:

Ἀγαθῇ τύχῃ.
Θεῷ Μηνὶ
Δωλανῷ
δῶρον
Κρέττιος
Μαρκιανός.

The epithet Δωλανός is new, and according to Şahin's indication, no. 35 of his collection (I have not yet been able to consult it in full), the Δωλανοί are a group of people known from two sarcophagus inscriptions of Nicomedeia.

The inscription is valuable in attesting Men-worship from an area where it had not previously been attested.

Şahin, *op. cit.*, nos. 67 and 68 also may be connected with Men-cult, as they bear a crescent, and no. 72 has a fragmentary inscription in which it may be possible to restore Men's name.

A 8. A stele with lugged bottom, now in museum of Izmit, but reportedly from area of Manisa.

Dimensions: unavailable.

> Bibliography: To be published in a forthcoming article by Elmar Schwertheim in *Istanbuler Mitteilungen*.

Under the top moulding, the stone bears a relief field, showing, to viewer's left, Men standing with pine-cone. His l. hand is upraised to hold a staff, which was apparently indicated either in perishable material or in paint. To viewer's right, a female divinity standing, with a polos on her head, a drum or tambourine in her r. hand, and a round object in her l. Under the relief field there is the following inscription:

Κατ' ἐπίπνοιαν Διὸς Κιλ-
λαμενηνοῦ Ἀρχελάου
κώμη Μηνὸς τέκουσαν   161-2 A.D.
καὶ Μῆναν Τύραννον καθι-
έρωσαν ἔτους σμς' μη(νὸς)
Πανήμου.

I reserve further discussion of this interesting piece until after Dr. Schwertheim's article has appeared.

A 9. *Serivada?*: Çiftlik, near Kizil Ören, Turkey (North of Açil Göl, ancient *Anaua Limne*)

Block of marble, built into wall of local tea-house. First seen by Kunibert Bering and Dieter Salzmann in June/July 1971.

Dimensions: Height 35.5 cm., width 32.5 cm., thickness less than 30 cm.

Bibliography: K. Bering and D. Salzmann, *Zeitschrift für Papyrologie und Epigraphik*, XIV, 1974, pp. 259-260.

The stone, which apparently served as a statue-base, bears the following inscription:

```
   Ἀπολλώνιος Με-
   νελάου τοῦ ἱερέος          100-101 A.D.
   καὶ Ἀμία ἡ γυνὴ αὐ-
   τοῦ καὶ Μενέλαος
 5 ὁ υἱὸς αὐτοῦ τῷ δή-
   μῳ τῷ Σεριουαδέ-
   ων παρὰ ἑαυτῶν
   ἀνέθηκαν Μῆνα
   Πατάλαον, ἔτους
10 ρπε´, Μ )( Γ
```

Professor Louis Robert has informed me by letter that he knows of an inscription from Phrygia that confirms the epigraphical attestation of Καμαρείτης as an epithet for Men, otherwise known only from coins of Nysa and restored in no. 56. Cf. *Laodicée du Lycos, Le Nymphée*, Quebec and Paris, 1969, p. 297, note 5.

Mr. Thomas Drew-Bear informs me that he knows of a letter of Eumenes II, into which a mention of a temple of Men has been restored. This should be very interesting when it is properly published. I have been shown in the storerooms of the Istanbul Archaeological Museum a marble bust and a terracotta of Men, as well as an altar portraying Men on one side. It is to be hoped that all these items will eventually be published.

II. *Old Material*

From the first volume of the Corpus I excluded (although I

perhaps should have mentioned them among the Dubia) the following inscriptions, because the presence of Attis Menotyrannus in them is attested only from old and unreliable copies, in the first two cases, and by dint of heavy restoration in the third. Now, however, further study of the historical context of these inscriptions has convinced me that I should at least make mention of them here. All are from Rome.

AD 2. Stone of uncertain description and dimensions. Presumably copied by Cyriacus of Ancona (ca. 1391-1457). Now lost.

Partial bibliography: *CIL*, VI, 508; Dessau, *ILS*, 4146; R. Duthoy, *The Taurobolium*, Leiden, 1969, p. 17, no. 21; G. S. R. Thomas, *Revue Belge*, 49, 1971, p. 55 ff.

The stone bears the following inscription:

Potentiss(imis) Diis [M(atri) D(eum) M(agnae) I(daeae) et At]
ti Menotyranno . . . .
Serapias h(onesta) f(emina) sacr(ata) [Deum]
Matris et Proserpinae
taurobolium criobol(ium) caerno
perceptum per Fl. Antoin
um Eustochium sac(erdotem) Phryg(em)
max(imum) praesentib(us) et tradentib(us)
c(larissimis) v(iris) ex ampliss(imo) et sanctiss(imo)
coll(egio) XVvir(orum) s(acris) f(aciundis) die XIII kal(endas)
Maias Cerealibus D(ominis) N(ostris)
Constantino Max(imo) Aug(usto) V et
Licinio Iun(iore) Caes(are) co(n)s(ulibu)s.

This inscription is dated April 19, 319 A.D., and if genuine is far the earliest in this series of inscriptions.

AD 3. A large altar described as follows by Duthoy from the *CIL*: "Magna ara mutilata. In quattuor angulis superioribus tauri caesi iacent; in sinistro latere aries ad pinum, in qua tympanum est; a dextris ad pinum taurus, ex qua pedum, fistulae, mitra pendent; a tergo faces lucentes transversae decussatim." Apparently first copied by Martin Smetius, active 1545-1551, but the fullest copy is by the notorious falsifier, Ligorius. Now lost. Dimensions unknown.

The stone bears the following inscription:

> Partial bibliography: *CIL*, VI, 511; Vermaseren, *CIMRM*, no. 522; F. Buecheler and E. Lommatzsch, *Carmina Latina Epigraphica*, Leipzig, 1895-1926, no. 1529; Duthoy, *op. cit.*, p. 19, no. 24.

M(atri) D(eum) M(agnae) Idaeae et Attidi Menoturanno
    S(ancto)
nobilis in causis forma celsusq(ue) Sabinus
hic pater Invicti mystica victor habet
sermo . . . . . duos reservans
consimiles aufest . . . .
et veneranda movet Cibeles Triodeia signa
augentur meritis simbola tauroboli
Ruf(ius) Caeoni(us) Cae(oni) Sabini f(ilius) v(ir) c(larissimus)
    p(ontifex) m(aior) hierof(anta) d(eae) Hecat(ae) aug(ur)
pub(licus) p(opuli) r(omani) Q(uititium) pater sacror(um)
    Invicti Methrae tauroboliatus
M(atris) D(eum) M(agnae) Id(aeae) et Attidis Minoturani et
    aram IIII id(us) Mart(ias)
Gratiano V et Merobaude consulibus dedicabit.
Antiqua generose domo cui regia Vestae
Pontifici felix sacrato militat igne
Idem augur triplicis cultor venerande Dianae
Persidiciq(ue) Mithrae antistes Babilonie templi
Tauroboli q(ue) simul magni dux mistice sacri

March 12, 377 A.D.

AD 4. An altar described by Duthoy from the CIL as follows: "Ara rudis ac male habita; superne arietes quinque, singuli scilicet in singulis angulis atque unus in fronte mactati iacent; in latere dextro stat aries sub pinu; a qua tympanum, fitulae compactae, et crotala dependent; in sinistro taurus stat sub altera pinu, a qua pedum et singulares fistulae duae suspensae sunt; a tergo sunt faces transversae." Apparently first copied by Martin Smetius. Now lost.

Dimensions unknown.

Partial bibliography: *CIL*, VI, 512; Dessau, *ILS*, 4154; Duthoy, *op. cit.*, p. 19, no. 25; L. Vidman, *Sylloge inscriptionum religionis Isiacae et Sarapiacae*, no. 447.

The stone bears the following inscription:

[M(atri) D(eum) M(agnae) I(daeae) et Attidi Menotyranno Dis Magnis e]t
[t]u[t]atoribus suis
Ceionius Rufius Volu[si]
anus v(ir) c(larissimus) et inlustr[is]
ex vicario Asie et Ceio
ni Rufi Volusiani v(iri) c(larissimi)
et inlustris ex prefecto [pre]
torio et ex prefecto ur [bi]
et Cecine Lolliane clar[issi]
me et inlustris femin[e]
Deae Isidis sacerdotis fi[lius]
iterato viginti annis exp[le]
tis taurobolii sui aram constitu [it]
et consecravit X kal(endas) Iun(ias) D(omino) N(ostro) Va[len]
tiniano Aug(usto) IIII et Neoterio c[o(n)s(ulibu)s.]

May 23, 390 A.D.

The exact relationship of the Lycaonian sepulchral inscriptions to Men-cult is problematical, and they, like the Attis Menotyrannus inscriptions, represent a puzzling peripheral area. The reading and interpretation of our no. 155 seemed assured by the observation of H. Swoboda et al., *Denkmäler aus Lykaonien, Pamphylien und Isaurien* (Prague, 1935), p. 18 until W. M. Calder's reinterpretation appeared in *MAMA*, VIII, no. 234a. He wishes to read the following for lines 7-8, and says that there is no room for other letters than those preserved at the end of line 7:

ἐνορκῶ τρὶς θ'
Μῆνας ἀνεπιλύτους

He bases his interpretation on two other inscriptions. Although I excluded them from CMRDM I, I have decided to include them here among the Addenda to the Dubia, not so much because I doubt Calder's readings, although not all letters appear clearly on the photograph, but because I do question whether these inscriptions, on Calder's interpretation at any rate, have anything meaningful to do with the god Men.

Savatra: Yali Banat, Turkey

AD 5. Five fragments of a sarcophagus lid, first seen by H. S. Cronin in 1901.
Dimensions: Height 59 cm., length 1.96 m., depth 93 cm.

> Bibliography: H. S. Cronin, *JHS*, XXII, 1902, p. 373, no. 127; W. M. Calder, *MAMA*, VIII, p. 42, no. 234; L. Robert, *Hellenica*, XIII, 1965, p. 38 and p. 242.

Under the effigy of the deceased, on the right side of the sarcophagus lid, together with a decoration of crescents alternately upside-down and right-side-up, there is the following inscription:
(I follow Calder's restoration, with a few additional suggestions of my own).

Κ. Ἰουλίττῃ γυναικὶ παναρέτῳ [....φιλ]άνδρῳ [....]ηι Στρατονείκη ἡ μήτηρ αὐτῆς καὶ Κ. Κέλ[σος ....]τ[....] καὶ ἑαυτῷ ὁ Κέλσος μόνοις τὴν λάρνακα μ[νήμης ἕνεκεν. Ἐνορκοῦμεν δὲ τ]ρὶς ἐννέα Μῆνας καταχθονίους μηδένα μ[ετὰ ἡμᾶς ἐπεισενεχθῆναι εἰ μή....] ἄνδρα.

Area of ancient *Perta*(?): Zengicek, Turkey

AD 6. Stele, broken at top. Known since 1934.
Dimensions: Height 92 cm.: width 41 cm.

> Bibliography: W. M. Calder, MAMA, VIII, p. 42, no. 234b.

The stone bears the following inscription:

[.......ὅς]
[δ' ἂν ἀδικήσῃ]
[τὴν στήλην]
ταύτην ἕ[ξει]
κεκολωμέν[ους]
Μῆνας αἰνέα

Calder did not copy the inscription himself, nor are we informed who did, except that the copier indicates room for only two letters lost at the end of the next-to-last line. That fact would shed considerable doubt on the restoration, as Calder admits.

AD 7. Finally the following was omitted from *CMRDM*, I, in what now seems to me to be excessive distrust of W. M. Ramsay, although he is a very easy scholar to distrust excessively:

A roughly-carved stone chair, found in 1912 in a structure adjoining the sanctuary of Men Askaenos above Pisidian Antioch. Dimensions unavailable.

Bibliography: W. M. Ramsay, *ABSA*, XVIII, 1911-12, p. 49; Lane I, pp. 41-42.

Ramsay read the following inscription on the chair, the first three lines being on the back, the last two below the seat:

Μηνὶ εὐχὴν
Μενέλαος
Ἀττάου
τοῦ καὶ
Κάρπου

As I stated, Lane I, p. 42, note 150, this inscription was no longer to be read in such detail in 1961, but all that could be made out was Μενε | αττα | Κάρπου. For dedications of furniture to Men, see no. 255; for the name Κάρπος, no. 253. (I still see no reason for reconsidering my rejection as having nothing demonstrable to do with Men-cult of the other inscription discussed in the same note, Ramsay, *JHS*, L, 1930, p. 274-75.)

PLATES

PLATE I

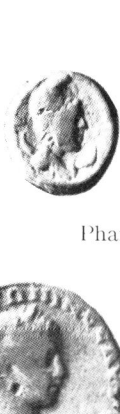

Pharnaceia 1   Gangra-Germanicopolis 1

Bithynium-Claudiopolis 1   Juliopolis 1

Juliopolis 2   Juliopolis 3

Juliopolis 4   Juliopolis 5

Juliopolis 6   Juliopolis 7

PLATE II

Juliopolis 8

Juliopolis 9

Juliopolis 10

Juliopolis 11

Juliopolis 12

Juliopolis 13

Juliopolis 14

Juliopolis 15

Juliopolis 16

Juliopolis 17

PLATE III

Elaia Aeolidis 1   Elaia 2

Magnesia on the
Maeander 1   Magnesia 2

Magnesia 3   Magnesia 4

Magnesia 5   Magnesia 6

Magnesia 7   Magnesia 8

PLATE IV

PLATE V

Bageis 1

Bageis 1 var.

Bageis 2

Bageis 3

Gordus-Julia 1

Gordus-Julia 2

Gordus-Julia 3

Gordus-Julia 4

Gordus-Julia 5

Gordus-Julia 6

Plate VI

Gordus-Julia 7

Gordus-Julia 8

Maeonia 1

Maeonia 2

Nysa 1

Nysa 2

Nysa 3

Nysa 4 (Paris)

Nysa 4 (Cambridge)

PLATE VII

Nysa 5

Nysa 6

Nysa 7

Nysa 8

Nysa 9

Nysa 10

Nysa 11

PLATE VIII

Nysa 12

Nysa 13

Nysa 14

Nysa 15

PLATE IX

Nysa 16

Nysa 17

Nysa 18   Nysa 19

Nysa 20   Nysa 22

PLATE X

Nysa 23 Nysa 24

Nysa 25

Nysa 26

Nysa 27

PLATE XI

Nysa 28

Nysa 29

Nysa 30

Nysa 31

PLATE XII

Nysa 32

Nysa 33

Nysa 34

Nysa 35

Nysa 36

Nysa 37

Nysa 38

Nysa 39

Nysa 40

PLATE XIII

Nysa 41

Nysa 42

Nysa 43

Saitta 1   Saitta 2

Plate XIV

Saitta 3

Saitta 4

Saitta 5

Saitta 6

Saitta 7

Saitta 8

Saitta 9

PLATE XV

Saitta 10

Saitta 11

Saitta 12

Saitta 13

Plate XVI

Saitta 14

Saitta 15

Saitta 16

Saitta 17

PLATE XVII

Saitta 18

Sardis 1

Sardis 2

Sardis 3

Sardis 4

Sardis 5

Sardis 6

Sardis 7

Sardis 8

PLATE XVIII

Sardis 9 Sardis 10

Sardis 11 Sardis 12

Sardis 13 Silandus 1

Silandus 2 Silandus 3

PLATE XIX

Silandus 4

Aphrodisias 1

Attouda 1

Attouda 2

Attouda 3

Cidrama 1

Trapezopolis 1

Trapezopolis 2

Trapezopolis 3

Trapezopolis 4

PLATE XX

Trapezopolis 5

Accilaeum 1

Alia 1

Alia 2

Alia 3

Alia 4

Alia 5

Alia 6

Alia 7

Apameia 1

PLATE XXI

Cibyra 1

Cibyra 2

Cibyra 3

Cibyra 4

Cibyra 5

Colossae 1

Colossae 2

Eriza 1

Grimenothyrae 1

Plate XXII

Grimenothyrae 2

Grimenothyrae 3

Grimenothyrae 4

Hadrianopolis 1

Hadrianopolis 2

Hadrianopolis 3

Hierapolis 1

Hierapolis 2

Hierapolis 3

Hierapolis 4

PLATE XXIII

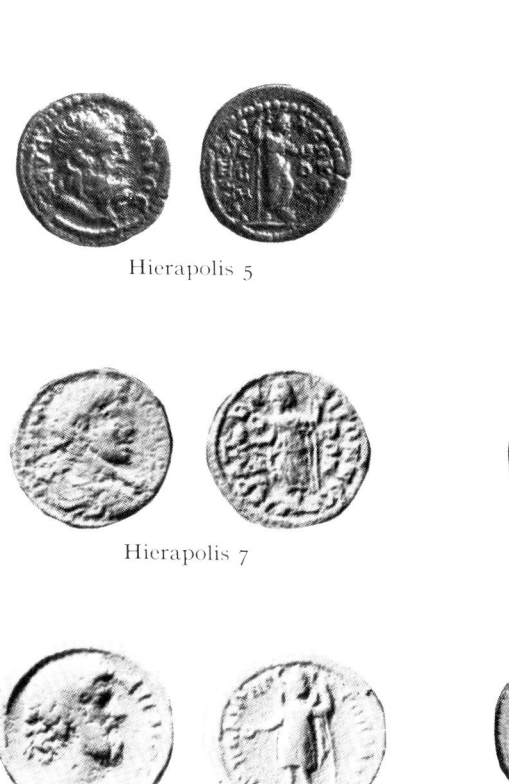

Hierapolis 5 · Hierapolis 6

Hierapolis 7 · Hierapolis 8

Hieropolis 1 · Hieropolis 2

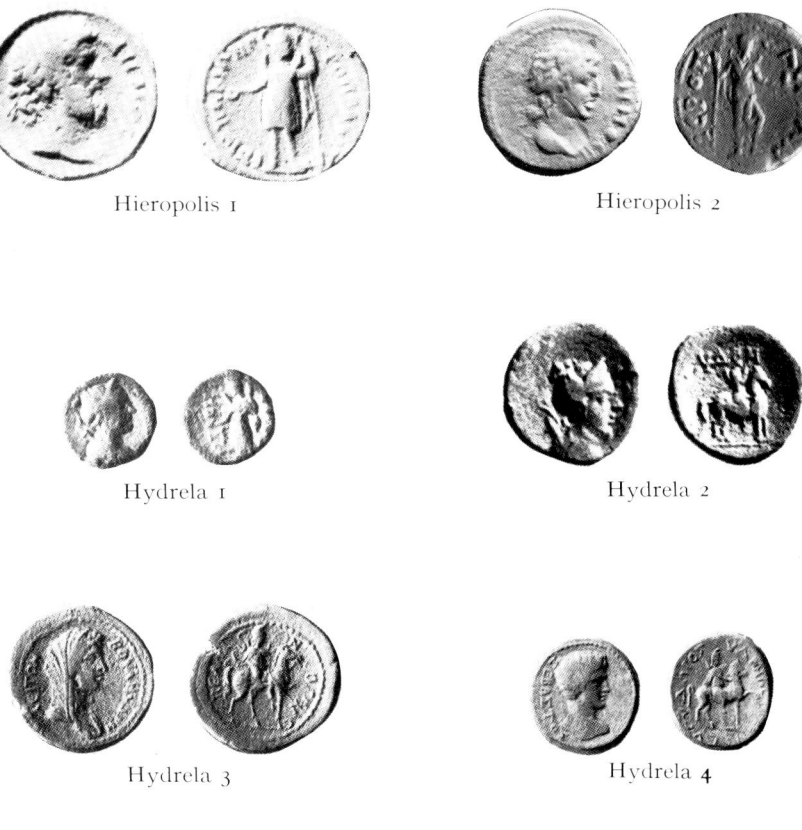

Hydrela 1 · Hydrela 2

Hydrela 3 · Hydrela 4

PLATE XXIV

Hydrela 5   Hyrgaleis 1

Julia 1   Julia 2

Julia 3   Julia 4

Laodiceia 1   Laodiceia 2

Laodiceia 3   Laodiceia 4

PLATE XXV

Laodiceia 5

Laodiceia 6

Metropolis 1   Metropolis 2

Metropolis 3

Midaeum 1

Plate XXVI

Paleobeudus 1

Philomelium 1

Philomelium 2

Philomelium 3

Prymnessus 1

Prymnessus 2

Sebaste 1

Sebaste 2

Sebaste 3

Sebaste 4

PLATE XXVII

Sebaste 5

Siblia 1   Siblia 2

Siblia 3   Siblia 4

Siblia 5   Synnada 1

Synnada 2   Synnada 3

Plate XXVIII

Temenothyrae 1

Temenothyrae 2

Temenothyrae 3

Temenothyrae 4

Temenothyrae 5

Temenothyrae 6

Temenothyrae 7

PLATE XXIX

Temenothyrae 8

Temenothyrae 9

Temenothyrae 10

Temenothyrae 11

Plate XXX

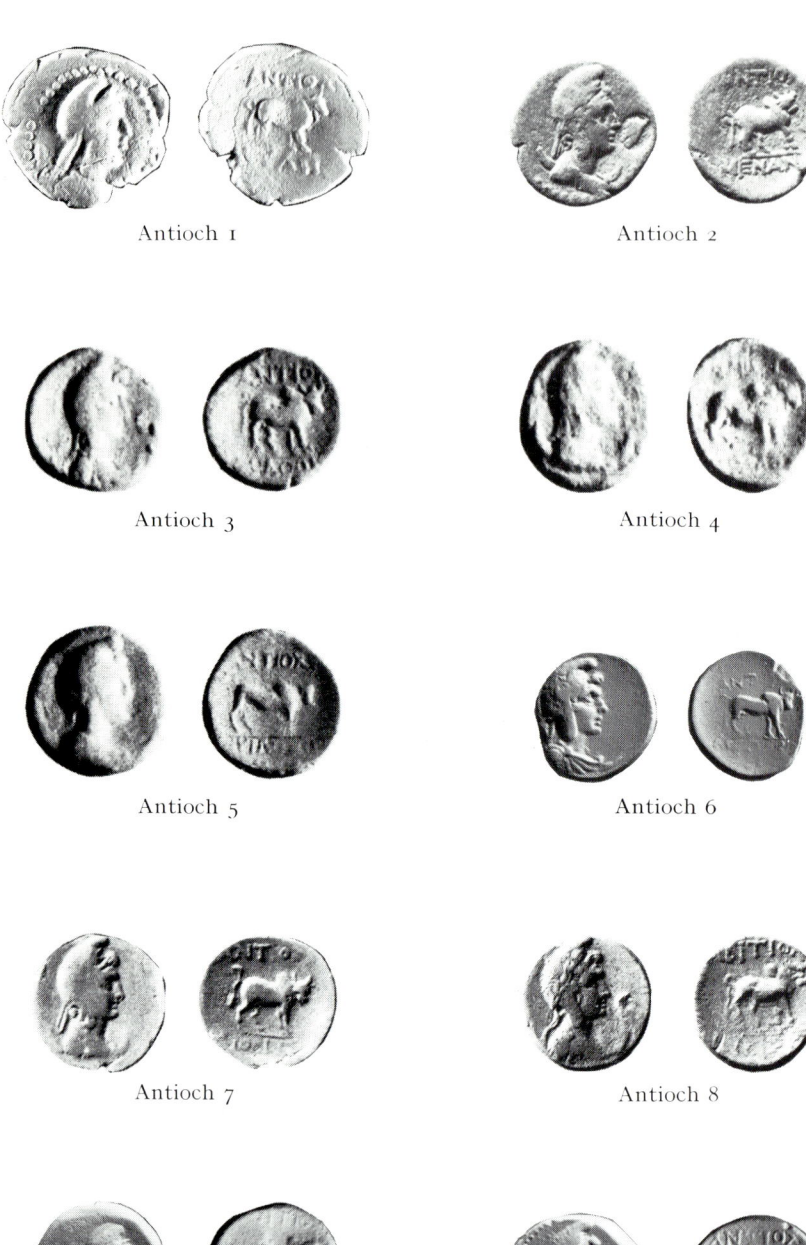

Antioch 1

Antioch 2

Antioch 3

Antioch 4

Antioch 5

Antioch 6

Antioch 7

Antioch 8

Antioch 9

Antioch 10

PLATE XXXI

Antioch 11

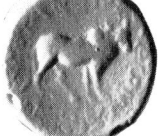

Antioch 12

Antioch 13

Antioch 14

Antioch 15

Antioch 16

Antioch 17

Antioch 18

Antioch 19

Antioch 20

Plate XXXII

Antioch 21

Antioch 22

Antioch 23

Antioch 24

Antioch 25

Antioch 26

Antioch 27

Antioch 28

Antioch 29

Antioch 30

PLATE XXXIII

Antioch 31

Antioch 32

Antioch 33

Antioch 34

Antioch 35

Antioch 36

Antioch 37

Antioch 38

Antioch 39

Antioch 40

Plate XXXIV

Antioch 41

Antioch 42

Antioch 43

Antioch 44

Antioch 45

Antioch 46

Antioch 47

Antioch 48

Antioch 49

Antioch 50

PLATE XXXV

Antioch 51

Antioch 52

Antioch 53

Antioch 54

Antioch 55

PLATE XXXVI

Antioch 56

Antioch 57

Antioch 58  Antioch 59

Antioch 60
Apollonia Pisidiae 1

Apollonia Pisidiae 2

PLATE XXXVII

Ariassus 1

Baris 1 Baris 2

Baris 3 Baris 4

Baris 5 Baris 6

Baris 7 Colbasa 1

Plate XXXVIII

Colbasa 2   Conana 1

Conana 2   Conana 3

Conana 4   Lysinia 1

Olbasa 1   Olbasa 2

Olbasa 3   Olbasa 4

PLATE XXXIX

Palaeopolis 1

Palaeopolis 2

Palaeopolis 3

Palaeopolis 4

Pappa-Tiberia 1

Parlais 1

Parlais 2

Parlais 3

Parlais 4

Parlais 5

PLATE XL

Parlais 6

Parlais 7

Parlais 8

Parlais 9

Prostanna 1

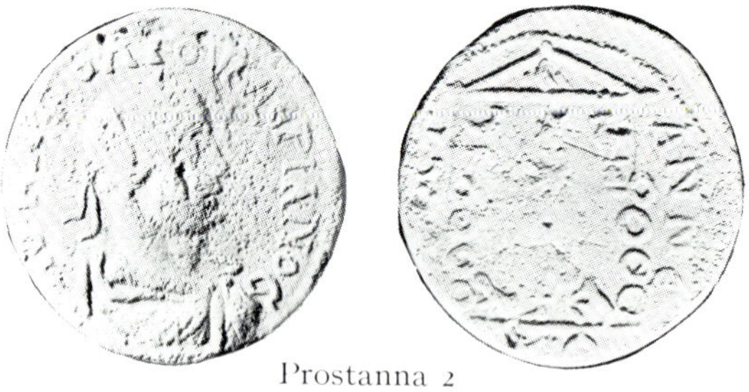

Prostanna 2

Sagalassus 1

Sagalassus 2

PLATE XLI

Sagalassus 3

Sagalassus 4

Sagalassus 5

Sagalassus 6

Sagalassus 7

Sagalassus 8

Sagalassus 9

Sagalassus 10

Sagalassus 11

Sagalassus 12

Plate XLII

Sagalassus 13

Sagalassus 14

Sagalassus 15

Sagalassus 16

Sagalassus 17

Sagalassus 18

Sagalassus 19

Sagalassus 20

Sagalassus 21

Sagalassus 22

PLATE XLIII

Sagalassus 23   Sagalassus 24

Sagalassus 25

Sagalassus 26

Sagalassus 27

PLATE XLIV

Seleuceia 1

Seleuceia 2

Seleuceia 3

Seleuceia 4

Seleuceia 5

Seleuceia 6

Seleuceia 7

Seleuceia 8

Seleuceia 9

Seleuceia 10

PLATE XLV

Seleuceia 11 Seleuceia 12

Seleuceia 13 Seleuceia 14

Sibidunda 1 Timbrias 1

Timbrias 2 Timbrias 3

Timbrias 4 Attaleia 1

Plate XLVI

Attaleia 2   Sillyon 1

Sillyon 2

Sillyon 3   Sillyon 4

Sillyon 5

Sillyon 6

PLATE XLVII

Sillyon 7

Sillyon 8

Sillyon 9

Sillyon 10

Plate XLVIII

Sillyon 11

Sillyon 12

Sillyon 13

Sillyon 14

Sillyon 15

Sillyon 16 Sillyon 17

PLATE XLIX

Sillyon 18

Sillyon 19

Sillyon 20

Sillyon 21

PLATE L

Sillyon 22 Sillyon 23

Sillyon 24

Sillyon 25

Sillyon 26 Sillyon 27

Sillyon 28

PLATE LI

Sillyon 29

Sillyon 30

Sillyon 31

Sillyon 32

Sillyon 33

Sillyon 34

Sillyon 35

Sillyon 36

Plate LII

Sillyon 37  Sillyon 38

Sillyon 39

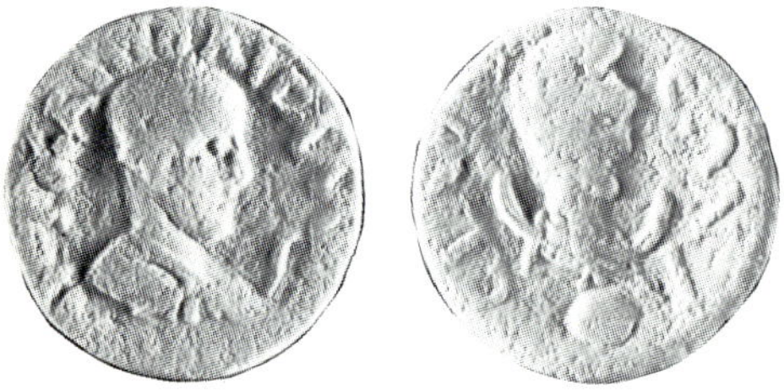

Sillyon 40  Sillyon 41

Sillyon 42

Sillyon 43

Sillyon 44

PLATE LIII

Sillyon 45

Sillyon 46

Sillyon 47

Sillyon 48

PLATE LIV

Sillyon 49

Sillyon 50

Sillyon 51

Sillyon 52

Plate LV

Sillyon 53 Sillyon 54

Galatia 1 Galatia 2

Galatia 3 Galatia 4

Galatia 5

Galatia 6 Galatia 7

PLATE LVI

Galatia 8

Ancyra 1   Ancyra 2

Ancyra 3

Ancyra 4   Ancyra 5

PLATE LVII

Ancyra 6

Ancyra 7

Ancyra 8 Ancyra 9

Ancyra 10 Ancyra 11

Ancyra 12 Ancyra 13

Plate LVIII

Ancyra 14　　　　　　　Ancyra 15

Uncertain, perhaps　　　　　Germe 1
Ancyra

Pessinus 1　　　　　　　Pessinus 2

Pessinus 3

Pessinus 4

PLATE LIX

Laodiceia ad Libanum 1

Laodiceia ad Libanum 2

Laodiceia ad Libanum 3

Laodiceia ad Libanum 4

Imperial Cistophori

Plate LX

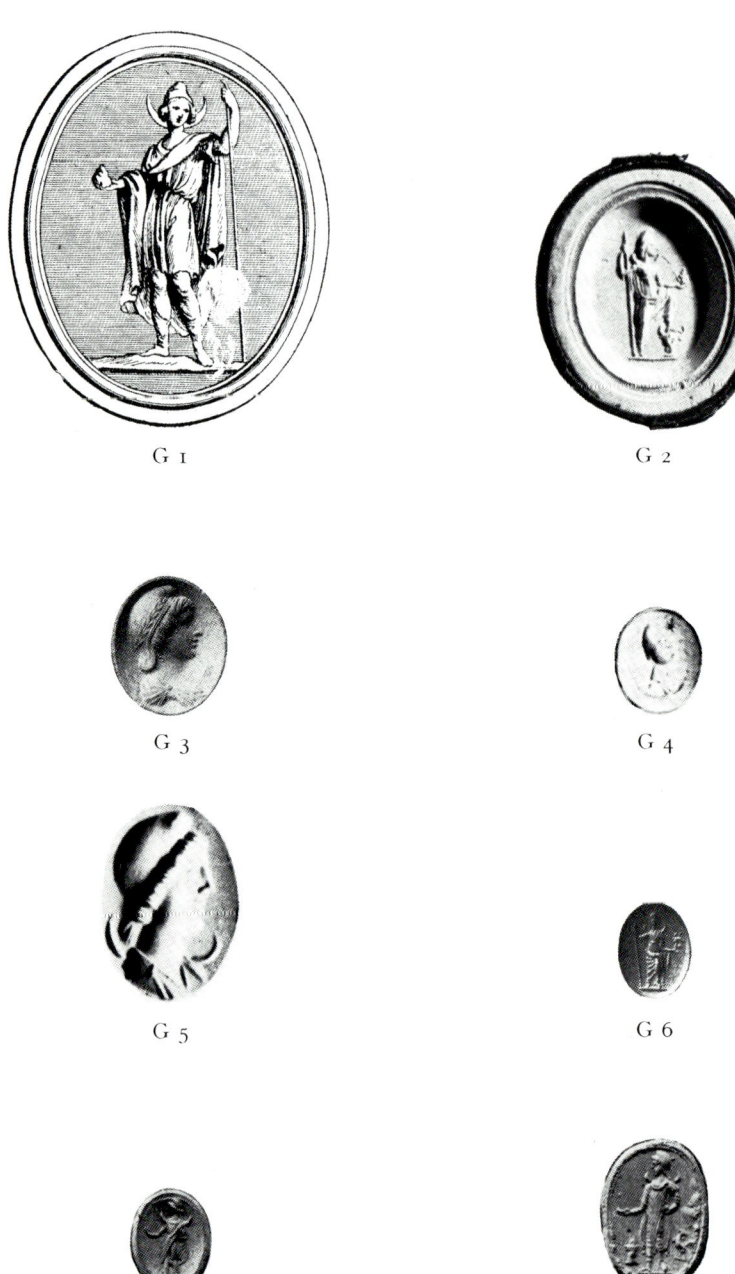

PLATE LXI

G 9

G 10

G 11

G 12

G 13

Plate LXII

PLATE LXIII

Plate LXIV

G 16

G 17

G 18

G 19

ADDENDA TO
PLATES OF VOLUME I

ADDENDA

Volume I, No. 163
(see p. 172)

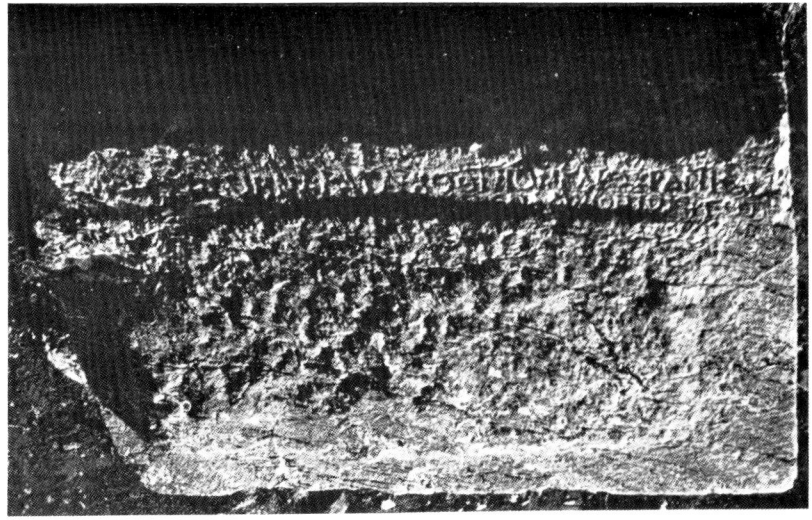

(A 5)

ADDENDA

(A 6) Fig. 1

ADDENDA

(A 6) Fig. 2

ADDENDA

(A 7)

(A 9)

ADDENDA

ADDENDA

(AD 5)

ADDENDA

(AD 6)

Plate from Hildesheim (see. p. 169)

Remarks: The traditional location of *Sibidunda* is shown on the map, but it is more probably to be found at Zivint, between *Olbasa* and *Ariassus*. See G. E. Bean, *Anatolian Studies*, 1960, pp. 68-69.